A FAITH FOR YOU

A FAITH FOR YOU

by R. C. Chalmers

JOHN KNOX PRESS
RICHMOND, VIRGINIA

Library of Congress Catalog Card Number: 62-8223

First published in 1960, under the title *A Gospel to Proclaim,*
by The Ryerson Press, Toronto
First United States edition, John Knox Press, 1962

DEDICATED TO

The Officers and Members of
The National Council of
The Young People's Union of
The United Church of Canada,
1958
with joy and gratitude.

v

CONTENTS

CHAPTER ONE / *Revelation*

PAGE

1. Elemental Religion 3

2. Counterfeit Religions 4

3. The Gospel 5

4. Faith 5

5. The Meaning of Revelation 6

6. What God Reveals 8

7. The Media of Revelation 9

    (i) Jesus Christ 9

    (ii) Nature 10

    (iii) History 12

    (iv) The Moral Nature of Man 12

8. The Record of Revelation: the Bible 13

9. The Finality of Christ's Revelation 15

10. Man's Response to God's Revelation 17

CHAPTER TWO / *Incarnation*

1. The Meaning of the Incarnation 21

2. Jesus of Nazareth, the Son of God 22

3. Jesus the Man 23

4. The Significance of Jesus' Human Life 25

5. Jesus Christ, the Divine Lord 27

vii

6. Doctrines that Witness to Christ's Lordship 28

  (i) The Virgin Birth 28

  (ii) The Word 29

  (iii) The Self-Emptying of Christ 30

7. The Reality of the Incarnation 31

8. The Decisive Question 32

9. Life Means Christ 33

CHAPTER THREE / *Reconciliation*

1. Introduction 37

2. Man and His Sin 39

  (i) The Meaning of Sin 39

  (ii) Sin as Estrangement 41

  (iii) The Consequences of Sin 41

  (iv) The Good News of the Gospel . . . 42

  (v) The Means of Reconciliation . . . 43

3. The Problem of Evil 46

  (i) Some Aspects of the Problem . . . 46

  (ii) The Devil 48

  (iii) The Suffering of the Righteous . . . 49

  (iv) The Cross and Suffering 50

4. Debtors to Divine Grace 52

5. The Call to Service 55

CHAPTER FOUR / *Resurrection*

1. The Significance of the Resurrection . . . 59

2. The New Testament Witness to the Resurrection . . 61

3. The Resurrection of the Body 63

4. The Consequences of the Resurrection 65

5. The Challenge of the Resurrection 69

6. The Ascension 71

CHAPTER FIVE / *Communion*

1. Introduction 75

2. The Nature and Work of the Holy Spirit . . . 75

3. The Trinity 77

4. The Fellowship of the Spirit 79

5. The Church and Pentecost 81

6. The Marks of the Church 82

    (i) Unity 82

    (ii) Holiness 83

    (iii) Catholicity 84

    (iv) Apostolicity 84

7. The Means of Grace 85

    (i) Worship 86

    (ii) Preaching and the Sacraments 86

    (iii) Baptism 87

    (iv) The Lord's Supper 88

CHAPTER SIX / *Consummation*

1. Introduction 91

2. The Christian Hope 91

3. The Kingdom of God 92

4. The Return of Christ 94

5. The Last Judgment 97

PAGE

6. The Final Destiny of the Righteous 99

   (i) Eternal Life 99

   (ii) Heaven 100

7. The Final Destiny of the Unrighteous 101

8. The Consummation of the Kingdom 103

CHAPTER SEVEN / *Commission*

1. Man's Need of Redemption 107

2. The Responsibility of the Church 108

3. The Authority of Christ 109

4. The Church Must Make Disciples 110

5. The Fourfold Mission of the Church 111

6. Factors in Making Disciples 113

7. Communion, Commitment and Commission 115

A FAITH FOR YOU

CHAPTER ONE

QUESTIONS FOR DISCUSSION

1 *If all men, as Calvin stated, have a "natural instinct for God," why do so many people live without faith in Him?*

2 *What are the chief "counterfeit religions" in the modern world?*

3 *Why is idolatry an ever-present danger?*

4 *Does the "good tidings" of Christianity mean that the gospel is always pleasing to us?*

5 *"We have but faith; we cannot know*
    For knowledge is of things we see" (Tennyson).
   Does faith give us knowledge? What can we see by faith?

6 *How can we determine what is and what is not God's revelation?*

7 *Why is revelation so important in Christianity?*

8 *Why is it necessary to stress that God acts in history? Is it not sufficient if He acts in heaven?*

9 *Why do we call the Bible "the Word of God"?*

10 *Should we obey conscience? Why not obey Christ?*

11 *What business have Christians interfering with the beliefs of adherents of other religions?*

12 *"To obey (the voice of the Lord) is better than sacrifice" (or worship) (1 Sam. 15: 22). Why? Should obedience to God and the worship of God be opposed to each other?*

Revelation

1 / ELEMENTAL RELIGION

"O Lord, thou hast searched me and known me" (Ps. 139: 1). This statement was once described by Dr. James Denney as "elemental religion." Such seeking and such knowledge by God is, according to the psalmist, the basis of self-knowledge and the heart of man's spiritual life. "Thou knowest when I sit down and when I rise up; thou discernest my thoughts from afar. Thou searchest out my path and my lying down, and art acquainted with all my ways. Even before a word is on my tongue, lo, O Lord, thou knowest it altogether" (Ps. 139: 2-4).

John Calvin affirmed his belief in this "elemental religion." He wrote in his famous *Institutes* that man has a "natural instinct" for God; that all people possess "some sense of a Deity because there has never been a country or family, from the beginning of the world, totally destitute of religion." He also believed that this fact proved that "some sense of divinity is inscribed on every heart."[1] In this respect Calvin is merely pointing to a truth noted by St. Paul, namely, that "ever since the creation of the world his (God's) invisible nature, namely his eternal power and deity, has been clearly perceived in the things that have been made" (Rom. 1: 20). Although sin has corrupted this sense

[1]John Calvin, *The Institutes of the Christian Religion.* 1. iii.

of deity in the mind of the natural man, St. Paul says that man is "without excuse" (Rom. 1: 20). This apostle also referred to this same phenomenon in human life when he preached at Athens and reminded the people "that in every way" he perceived they were "very religious" (Acts 17: 22). Few facts are better attested by history and anthropology than that man is a worshipping and believing creature.

It is in this solemn thought that God is seeking man, that God knows man and loves him, and that some elemental knowledge of God is inscribed in the heart of every man, that we have the foundation of man's religious life. It is not primarily in what man does but rather in what God has done and is doing for man that we discern the basis of true religion.

2 / COUNTERFEIT RELIGIONS

St. Paul (in Rom. 1: 21ff), Calvin and others have pointed out that man has perverted this religious sense and turned the primary disclosure of God in the soul into a lie. And in our day we have plenty of evidence of "ersatz" religions and cults that are counterfeits of the real thing. Men have forsaken the true God and worshipped false gods of state and power and self. When the true God goes the half-gods come. And this worship of anything other than God is idolatry. It is man's attempt to create a religion that will conform to his self-centredness. Such counterfeit religions give glory to man and not to God. Communism, for instance, is a form of secular religion which exalts man and the state. Materialism, which is devotion to material possessions and things, is also a form of idolatry. "Be appalled, O heavens, at this, be shocked, be utterly desolate, says the Lord, for my people have committed two evils: they have forsaken me, the fountain of living waters, and hewed out cisterns for themselves, broken cisterns, that can hold no water" (Jer. 2: 12, 13).

Man suffers from "an incurable god-sickness," states Karl Barth. He is the "god-intoxicated" creature. "My soul thirsts for God, for the living God" (Ps. 42: 2), cried the psalmist. Hence man is essentially a religious being. If he does not rely on the true God he will cling to idols. If he does not feed his soul "on angels' food" he will try to satisfy his soul's hunger on the husks of materialism. But the very fact that man will embrace some counterfeit religion, if he does not have the true one, is witness to the fundamental truth that man was made in the divine likeness (Gen. 1: 26) and only in His will can he find peace.

3 / THE GOSPEL

Accepting this truth of elemental religion, Christianity declares that it has a gospel to proclaim to men, a message to give to humanity which comes from God Himself. In contrast to elemental religion, the gospel is not general but specific; it is not abstract but personal; it is not vague but concrete.

The English word gospel is the translation of a Greek term which means "good tidings." It means "God-story," that is a story which comes from God. When Jesus came preaching He declared the gospel of the Kingdom or reign of God. But following His death and resurrection the Church came to see the gospel in terms of Jesus Christ Himself. So we read of "the gospel of Jesus Christ, the Son of God" (Mark 1: 1). Still later the term gospel became a technical designation of original Christianity. But the one thing of importance is that in the gospel God has delivered a message to all men whose culmination is to be found in Jesus Christ the Lord. Through Him God has addressed His truth to people of all ages. And this message and this truth is that in Jesus Christ God has "visited and redeemed his people" from their sin and granted to them the gift of the abundant life. It is this gospel which the Church is commissioned to proclaim. It is this declaration of "good tidings" which the Church has to offer to men.

4 / FAITH

But how is man to receive this gospel? It is received by faith. "For I am not ashamed of the gospel," writes St. Paul, "it is the power of God for salvation to every one who has faith, to the Jew first and also to the Greek" (Rom. 1: 16). Faith, according to Luther, is "God's wedding-ring," that which God gives us to bind us to Himself. Faith is always God-initiated and God-inspired. "For by grace you have been saved through faith; and this is not your own doing, it is the gift of God" (Eph. 2: 8). By faith we are enabled to appropriate the gospel of God's redeeming love. By faith we are strengthened to walk in newness of life.

Although the term faith is used in the New Testament to denote a body of teaching (e.g. 1 Tim. 6: 10), its chief meaning is that of trust in the person of Jesus Christ and only in a secondary and derivative sense as belief in teachings about Him. Faith is personal commitment to a person, the Lord of life. It is what Luther also called "throwing oneself on God." "I have been crucified with Christ," writes St. Paul, "it is no longer I who live, but Christ who lives in me; and the life I now live in the flesh I live by faith in the Son of God, who loved me and gave himself for me" (Gal. 2: 20).

But all discussion of the gospel and faith, and even of elemental religion, presupposes a prior action on the part of God, a divine self-disclosure upon which true religion must depend, a self-giving of the Father to sinful men. That is, we must give priority to revelation.

5 / THE MEANING OF REVELATION

In Christianity revelation is the correlative of faith. That is, we can only have faith in the Christian sense in that which is revealed, while revelation assumes a corresponding faith if its truth is to be apprehended by man.

The word "revelation" means "unveiling." Something that has been hidden has now been made manifest. And the very fact that there is a revelation depends entirely on God Who is the One Who wills and acts to make Himself known to man. Pascal puts into the mouth of God some words which tell us the meaning of revelation: "Thou wouldst not have sought me unless

I had already found thee." Even the vague sense of deity which Paul says is to be found among pagans (Rom. 1: 20) assumes some revelation which is only dimly understood by man.

Christianity stands or falls on this matter of revelation. If God has not made Himself known savingly in Jesus Christ, we have no gospel to offer men. Christianity is then only one of a number of religions, lacking power and vitality which God alone can supply. A religion without revelation is an empty shell: the form without the force, the shadow without the substance.

But revelation gives us a gospel, a message of good news from God to man. This is not a message of man's devising, nor the product of man's speculating. In the fulness of time God Himself appeared among men in the form of a man, the man Christ Jesus. Christ is the revealing fact upon which our faith is based. He is the life-giver in the gospel we proclaim. He is God's self-revelation to a sinful world.

In the New Testament revelation is always "the revelation of the mystery" (Rom. 16: 25), that is the disclosure of something "which was kept secret for long ages." Mystery (in the biblical sense) is not a riddle to which no answer can be found, or a story in which a secret is made plain and a mystery resolved in the last few pages. In the New Testament the term "mystery" indicates that something is disclosed which was previously obscure or hidden, and also that something still remains mysterious or secret. This is so because it is the mystery of God's nature with which we are dealing, and man's finite mind can never know all that there is to know about the Infinite God. Thus in revelation while something is unveiled of God's nature and purpose there is also something that remains veiled, something which the mind of man cannot fathom. So the revelation of the mystery of God does not dissolve all that is mysterious. Something more is known about God than heretofore, but something remains unknown. Revelation discloses, but revelation also conceals.

It was said of Lincoln by one of his contemporaries: "He is a great man and a great leader of men. I have known him for many years and I love him. But there is something mysterious about him." Perhaps this statement gives us a clue to the meaning of "the revelation of the mystery." This friend of Lincoln's knew Lincoln. He could describe him and tell much about him. Lincoln had "revealed" himself to his friend. But at the same time the mystery of Lincoln's personality was not dissolved. There was still an unknown something about Lincoln which even friendship could not discern. The more he knew of Lincoln the more he did not know about him. And if this can be so about our relations with friends on earth how much more is it true of our friendship with God! He reveals Himself to us in Christ through faith and love. But there is a mystery about His Being which will always remain. A god fully comprehended by reason is not the God and Father of our Lord Jesus Christ.

6 / WHAT GOD REVEALS

What does God impart through revelation? Not truths but the truth. Not a body of information, or a set of doctrines, or a list of propositions. These are at best only human expressions of the revelation. But in the revelation itself God gives nothing less than Himself. He not merely speaks; He comes. "God was in Christ" (2 Cor. 5: 19). William Temple wrote that "knowledge of God can be fully given to man only in a person, never in a doctrine."[2] In revelation God discloses His mind and nature and purpose in a very personal way. And because revelation is personal God reveals Himself to persons. "There is no revelation 'in general'," writes Paul Tillich; "revelation grasps an individual or a group, usually a group, through an individual."[3]

We are told in Scripture that the agent in revelation is the Word of God (e.g. John 1: 1-14). The Word of God is God in His outgoing love making Himself known to man, communicating His nature to man. The Word of God is "living and active, sharper than any two-edged sword, piercing to the division of soul and spirit, of joints and marrow, and discerning the thoughts and intentions of the heart" (Heb. 4: 12).

[2]William Temple, *Nature, Man and God*, p. 321.
[3]Paul Tillich, *Systematic Theology*, Volume 1, p. 111.

The Protestant Reformers of the sixteenth century used to speak of the Word of God manifesting Himself to men in three ways: through preaching, which is the Word of God spoken; through the Bible, which is the Word of God written; and through Jesus Christ, Who is the living Word of God. Jesus Christ is the Word made flesh and it is through Him that we are able to discern the reality of the Word in preaching and in the Scriptures.

We must beware of identifying the forms of revelation with the revelation itself. That would be a kind of idolatry, that is, the worship of something other than God. For that which God reveals, Himself, is always something more, something above and beyond the organs or forms in which the revelation comes to us. For example, God's Word comes to us through the Bible. But we must never identify the human words of a book, no matter how revered, with the Word of God Himself. There is a Word behind our human words, a Word which transcends them, corrects them, judges them, and which reminds us of Him with Whom we have to do, the God to Whom we are accountable.

7 / THE MEDIA OF REVELATION

The media of revelation are chiefly four in number:

(i) *Jesus Christ.* He is God's Word to men. Christians determine what is and what is not true revelation according to the disclosure which we find in Him. Knowledge of God apart from Him is vague at best. Some would say that apart from Christ we do not know God at all. (Such men believe that Christ speaks in a veiled manner in the authentic revelation of God in the Old Testament). It is in the light of Christ that we see the truth of God. It was by Christ's power that the worlds were framed (Heb. 11: 3) and in Him all things cohere (Col. 1: 17). It is Christ's life which is the light that enlightens every man who comes into the world (John 1: 9). Because of His primacy we must consider all other forms of revelation as dependent or secondary, for without Him we do not know what is and what is not revelation.

The important point to note here, briefly, is that God's revelation in Christ is remedial revelation. Christ and His forgiving love are "God's remedy for sin." "He is our peace, who has made us both one, and has broken down the dividing wall of hostility . . . and might reconcile us both to God in one body through the cross" (Eph. 2: 14-16). Christ reveals not merely to enlighten; He reveals in order to redeem. (Further consideration of who Jesus is and what He has done will be given in Chapters Two and Three).

(ii) *Nature.* One of Joseph Addison's hymns has these lines.

> The spacious firmament on high,
> With all the blue ethereal sky,
> And spangled heavens, a shining frame,
> Their great Original proclaim.

Addison was re-echoing the words of Psalm 8: "O Lord, our Lord, how majestic is thy name in all the earth" (v. 1).

It is well to note that Addison and the psalmist did not, strictly speaking, "find God in nature." They were devout, religious souls who knew God through a prior revelation to them in worship and the other means of grace and were thus able to see God in the things which He had made. They knew Him to be the Lord of all and thus they were able to discern the "skirts of His ways."

Since God is the Creator of nature it ought to be possible for a believer to see in His handiwork some token of His character. To one who has a deep religious faith the very order of nature speaks of God. He understands this order to be one more line of evidence which tells him of God's faithfulness. Nor does he draw any sharp line of demarcation between the works of God and say, in effect, God is "here" and at the same time imply that God in not "ther.." In some deep sense God is both "there" and "here." To the believer, therefore, all occurrences must be to some degree revelations of God. "Unless all existence is a medium of revelation, no particular revelation is possible . . . only if

God is revealed in the rising of the sun in the sky can He be revealed in the rising of the son of man from the dead."[4]

But, as William Temple also points out, no man can ever hope to contemplate the universe in its entirety, so that general revelation in the strict sense is impossible. What is possible is that having experienced this deeply personal revelation, through an encounter of faith in Jesus Christ, we are then able to see that this divine Lord has also made plain the being of the Almighty Father in His creation. Once we have known God in Christ we find it impossible to believe that God has severed Himself from that which He has made in such a manner as to "offer no revelation of Him at all."[5] Therefore we are able to say that while nature, in and of itself, has no revelation to give to the unbeliever, nevertheless to the believer, whose God is Creator as well as Redeemer, the things of nature speak to him, saying in effect, "the hand that made us is divine."

Moreover, since God is the Lord of creation we must beware of all tendencies in our thinking which set science and its discoveries over against God and His revelation. To the Christian, God makes His ways known in and through scientific means as well as in other ways. The man who is a Christian can also be a scientist. Science itself is based on a faith in the orderliness, dependability and unity of the world, upheld and sustained by one God. It is in a monotheistic (believing in one God) culture that science has grown and developed and given its best to man.

Since God is the Creator, He is sovereign in His own universe. He is the One Who makes it a universe, not a multiverse. "Either God is in the whole of nature, with no gaps, or he's not there at all."[6] Therefore we should cultivate that wholeness of outlook which sees God at work not only in things specifically religious but also in the world of nature around us. The gateway of the Cavendish Physical Laboratory at Cambridge University (named after the English chemist and physicist, Henry Cavendish) is

---

[4]William Temple, *Nature, Man and God*, p. 306.   [5]*Ibid*, p. 305.
[6]C. A. Coulson, *Science and Christian Belief*, p. 22.

adorned with these words: "The works of the Lord are great: sought out of all those that have pleasure therein" (Ps: 111: 2). Hence we can believe that "the earth is the Lord's and the fulness thereof" (Ps. 24: 1). For the Christian, therefore, "all life is sacramental; all nature is needed that Christ should be understood: Christ is needed that all nature should be seen as holy."[7]

(iii) *History*. God has revealed Himself to man in history, according to Christianity. "I am the Lord thy God, who brought you out of the land of Egypt" (Ex. 2: 2) is the witness of the Old Testament to this faith. And the heart of the New Testament message is that "the Word became flesh and dwelt among us" (John 1: 14). God came into history, therefore history has meaning.

By God's revelation in Christ something happened in history which is decisive for history. Henceforth all history is dated "before Christ" (B.C.) and "anno domini" (A.D.). The event of Christ is the turning point in history, explaining what happened before He came and interpreting all that has occurred since His advent. History thus becomes, for the Christian, His story. God's mighty acts in the pilgrimage of the children of Israel, in the appearance of the prophets and in the coming of Christ, Who discloses the true purpose of God in all events in time, remind us that we live in a universe of meaning because God is the God Whom Jesus Christ has revealed.

(iv) *The Moral Nature of Man*. If conscience does not "make cowards of us all," at least it bothers us to no end. Man is a moral creature. He realizes that some things are right and some things are wrong, even when he may not be too well aware of the distinction himself. Moreover, in "this age without standards," when moral imperatives seem to have lost their authority for many people, there is sufficient evidence to show that "the way of the transgressor is hard" (Prov. 13: 15), the transgressor being one who violates the moral commandments of God which are summarized in the Ten Commandments of

[7]*Ibid.*, p. 118.

Moses and the New Commandment of Christ (Ex. 20: 3ff and John 13: 34f).

Those who believe in Christ interpret this wonder of the moral nature of man as evidence that God is revealing Himself there also. God has not left Himself without a witness in the heart of man. He speaks. He calls. He judges. He condemns. He inspires. He guides. He empowers. And we who believe in Christ believe also that in and through the anxieties, frustrations and guilt of those who know Him not, as well as in the lives of those who acknowledge Him to be the Lord, God is at work through the power of the Holy Spirit, endeavouring through His mercy to win man into fellowship with Himself. Since we believe that God is at work in the hearts of all men, the Church goes forth to proclaim His good news, knowing that He will give the increase.

8 / THE RECORD OF REVELATION: THE BIBLE

The Bible holds a place of unique significance in Christianity. It is the record of God's revelation to man, the chief testimony to the mighty acts of God for us men and our salvation, culminating in the coming of Christ the Saviour.

It has been said that Protestants are "the people of a Book." Sometimes the Bible has been referred to as "the paper Pope." That the Bible has authority for Protestants is beyond question. And the reason why the Bible has authority in the realm of faith and morals is that in it we find Jesus Christ speaking to us as we find Him in no other place. Because of this fact it is more accurate to say that Protestants are "the people of a Person," since it is the authority of Christ which comes to us through this book. The Bible is Christ's witness. All that is in the Bible, as well as outside it, is judged by the Christian in the light of His life and teaching, His death and resurrection. As Luther said, the Bible is "the manger in which Christ lies."

When we speak of the Bible as the Word of God we mean that in and through the human words in this book God speaks to men

His saving Word; God makes Himself known; God reveals Himself as He does no place else. Moreover, the divine authority of the scriptures as the Word of God "is from the inward work of the Holy Spirit, bearing witness by and with the Word in our hearts," to quote the Westminster Confession of Faith. This Reformation teaching of the "inner witness of the Holy Spirit" in the believer's heart, causing the words of the Bible to bring to him a message from God, rules out all mechanical and wooden ideas of scriptural inspiration. Here, as elsewhere, God's revelation is personal.

To Protestants the Bible is an open book, since God has "more light and truth yet to break forth out of His holy Word." God is "not the God of the dead but the God of the living." This implies that His revelation is not static but dynamic, not closed but open.

This openness of revelation has led many people to believe in the idea of "progressive revelation" in scripture. However, neither God nor His revelation "progresses" in our human sense. Moreover, the phrase "progressive revelation" seems to imply that revelation is given in propositions or supernatural communiques from the Almighty rather than in personal self-giving to men in Christ. What some people endeavour to convey by means of this phrase, however, is that man's apprehension of God has developed. It is the one God in Christ Who "is the same yesterday and today and forever" (Heb. 13: 8), Who changes not, Who reveals Himself to men. But man's capacity for receiving and understanding God's revelation has varied from time to time.

Thus while the Bible reflects this variety of men's understanding of God and His will for them, it is nevertheless the same God Who reveals Himself in both Testaments. In the Old Testament He is the God of promise; in the New Testament the God of fulfilment. Christ did not come to cancel out the Old Testament but to bring to light its hidden glory. In this way He gives meaning to the whole of scripture, completing what was partial, fulfilling what was promised.

9/THE FINALITY OF CHRIST'S REVELATION

The gospel proclaims that the revelation of God in Jesus Christ is the climax and culmination of all revelation and therefore it is final. In Christ, and Christ alone, man is offered redemption. With the apostles we are constrained to affirm that "there is salvation in no one else, for there is no other name under heaven given among men by which we must be saved" (Acts 4: 12).

When we speak of revelation in Christ as final we mean that it is the norm or standard of all revelation. It is in His light that we see light. He is the court of appeal to which we turn for guidance in matters of faith and morals. Christ is the touchstone by which we judge the truth or falsehood of religion. Further, when through faith Christ claims us for His own, we know that He gives us a quality of life which we can find in no other way and from no other person.

To speak of God's revelation in Christ as final is not, however, to claim the same finality for Christianity itself, or the Church, or dogmas, creeds and liturgies. These are human expressions of the divine revelation, but the revelation itself transcends them. Therefore when we refer to the finality of the Christian revelation we must point to Christ Himself Who is the Truth.

To some people the claim that the Christian revelation is final sounds arrogant, narrow-minded, bigoted and uncharitable. Such folk believe that since there is truth in all religions no one religion has a priority over the others. For example, Arnold Toynbee says that "the heart of so great a mystery" as that of the being of God cannot "be reached by following one road only." He continues: "Even if it should prove to be true that the other higher religions have less of the truth in them than ours has, this would not mean that they have in them no truth at all; and the truth that they have may be truth that our own religion lacks."[8]

Such a statement shows a misunderstanding of the finality of

[8]Arnold Toynbee, *An Historian's Approach to Religion,* p. 297.

the Christian revelation. It assumes that the Christian revelation is given in a set of propositions instead of in a Person. It presupposes that we find the truth by comparing the teaching of Christianity with the teachings of other faiths.

What Toynbee and others overlook is that the Christian revelation is a revelation given to man by God in a series of unrepeatable historical events which have divine meaning. Man interprets this revelation by means of doctrines, but the revelation itself must not be confused with these doctrines. Truth is more fundamental than truths. Moreover, few Christians would say that there is no truth in other religions. What we do affirm is that whatever element of truth is to be found in other religions is already seen in Christ in a more complete and perfect manner. What can be lacking in Christ's love on the cross? What can compare with the power of His risen life? Further, we must not overlook the contradictions between the Christian revelation and the teachings of other faiths. For example, at the heart of the Christian revelation is belief in the Fatherhood of God; to Moslems this is unthinkable. To Christians Christ is God incarnate; to Moslems the incarnation implies the deification of man—the worst sort of blasphemy.

We may note in passing that we have final standards in other areas of life. We have, for example, classics in art, literature and music. The existence of these classics shows us that there is at least approximate finality in these areas of human expression. The classics refer to a perfection that is beyond them, even though this perfection is manifest in and through them. Moreover, finality in these fields does not prevent further creative expression of man's genius. Rather, such finality becomes a spur, an inspiration to creative painting, writing and composing. And if this approximate finality can be found in human culture, why should we think it impossible to see finality in the realm of divinity where the perfect One, God Himself, reveals Himself in a perfect manner?

To those who have been enlightened and redeemed by Christ, "who have tasted the heavenly gift, and have become partakers of the Holy Spirit, and have tasted the goodness of the Word of

God and the powers of the age to come" (Heb. 6: 4, 5), there is
no alternative: either Christ is Lord of all or He is not Lord
at all. We may refrain from commending to others as final any
present forms or expressions of Christianity. But we are constrained by faith and experience to commend Christ as God's
final revelation because we know that His love is none other
than the love of God Who has come to seek for sinful man until
He finds him.

C. F. Andrews was once asked: "How do you preach to a
Hindu?" Andrews replied: "I don't. I preach to a man."
Basically all men have the same needs because all men are made
in God's image and have "come short of His glory." Christ is
the only Mediator Who can meet man's needs and overcome His
sin. We see Who Christ is "through His benefits" and when we
receive these benefits we know that there is no other. "Lord, to
whom shall we go?" asked the disciples of Jesus in the days of
His flesh and we would re-echo their reply: "You have the words
of eternal life" (John 6: 68). When Thomas asked the question:
"Lord . . . how can we know the way?" Jesus made the reply
in terms that the Church has proclaimed in all ages: "I am the
way, and the truth, and the life; no one comes to the Father,
but by me" (John 14: 5-7).

10 / MAN'S RESPONSE TO GOD'S REVELATION

One of the outstanding features of the theology of Karl
Barth is its emphasis on the truth that God's revelation in Christ
demands a response from man. When God reveals Himself He
also constrains man to decide for Him. When God speaks man
must obey. This is the "existential" moment that is filled with
destiny. To hear the Word of God means that we must become
involved in the service of God. When we have "tasted the powers
of the age to come" we feel constrained to take up the tasks of
God in this present age. "Not every one who says to me, 'Lord,
Lord,' shall enter the kingdom of heaven," said Jesus, "but he
who does the will of my Father who is in heaven" (Matt 7: 21).
In the New Testament we read the story of the rich young

ruler who came running to Jesus to ask Him a question about finding eternal life, that is life that is abiding and rich in quality. He listened when Jesus said: "Sell all that you have, and give it to the poor, and you will have treasure in heaven; and come, follow me." But as we read on we learn that the rich young ruler's countenance fell "and he went away sorrowful" (Mark 10: 17-25). John Baillie's comment on this story is that the rich young ruler "could never again complain of the lack of revelation."[9]

Revelation is no longer our need. We fail at the point of response to God's revelation. We do not obey His voice when He calls to us. He speaks but we give little attention to what He says. We are preoccupied. God comes to us in Christ and while we may not dismiss Him or deny Him, we pass Him by even while we may mutter some words of appreciation about His fine teachings. As if all that Christ wanted was our appreciation? Or we may hope that He will call again at some more convenient season when we won't be quite so busy with temporal affairs and we will have time to chat with Him about "spiritual things." This is the worst of all blasphemies: treating the Almighty in a trivial way. Playing the game of "hide and seek" with the Saviour is only one more method of postponing the reply which we must inevitably make to the all-important question: "What shall I do with Jesus who is called Christ" (Matt. 27: 22)?

Escape from this "tremendous lover" is impossible. He pursues us even when we make our bed in hell. He finds us in places where we expect He would never come. "Just when we're safest" He intrudes into our hearts with the marks of the nail-prints in His hands. His love will not let us go. Therefore the one response we should make to this revelation of God in Christ is to give ourselves to Him in glad surrender, to be used in the service of His Kingdom and for His glory, saying with the prophet when he received his call, "Lord, Here I am! Send me" (Is. 6: 8)!

[9]John Baillie, *The Idea of Revelation in Recent Thought*, p. 141.

FOR FURTHER READING

GENERAL

Christian Doctrine, by John S. Whale
Introducing New Testament Theology, by A. M. Hunter
The Wonder of the Christian Gospel, by J. M. Shaw
A Faith to Proclaim, by James S. Stewart

ON THIS CHAPTER

The Idea of Revelation in Recent Thought, by John Baillie
Revelation and Response, by E. P. Dickie

CHAPTER TWO

QUESTIONS FOR DISCUSSION

1 *How do we know that Jesus Christ was God incarnate?*

2 *Jesus was the Son of God and we are the sons of men. What's the difference?*

3 *If Jesus Christ was God's "Only-begotten Son", were His temptations real?*

4 *How does a Christian measure the worth of a person?*

5 *"No one comes to the Father, but by me," said Jesus. Is this not a bigoted statement?*

6 *Is belief in the Virgin Birth an essential aspect of the gospel?*

7 *Isn't talk about Christ's two natures, divine and human, rather silly?*

8 *Why is the correct reply to the question, "What do you think of Christ" of such significance? Isn't it sufficient to believe in His teachings?*

9 *Can we know the real meaning of love apart from belief in Jesus Christ?*

10 *Why should faith in a person who lived long ago be so important? Would it not be better to have faith in several great people, past and present?*

11 *How can the life and teaching of One Who lived in an age when there were no radios, television sets, automobiles, atomic bombs, airplanes, etc., be of help to us who live in this complex world?*

12 *"Believe in the Lord Jesus, and you will be saved" (Acts 16: 31). What meaning does such a statement convey to the "man-in-the-street" today?*

Incarnation

1/THE MEANING OF THE INCARNATION

"The Word became flesh and dwelt among us, full of grace and truth" (John 1: 14). Only a Hebrew would write that. Greek thought was so saturated with a dualism between matter and spirit that it was inconceivable for many to believe that the divine life could be embodied in human form. But to the Hebrew, who believed that God the Creator loved matter, since He had made it, the affirmation that divinity could take life in humanity was something he could understand. As Augustine wrote: "If in the books of the Platonists (Greek thinkers) it was to be found that in the beginning was the Word, it was not found there that the Word became flesh and dwelt among us." It was left to Hebrew writers to record this greatest of all events in the history of man.

The word Incarnation means "in the flesh." In Christian theology it refers specifically to the fact that Jesus Christ embodied Himself in human form and came among men as a man. This means that the coming of Christ is the focal point of reference in all Christian thinking. By this event Christian theology, art, culture and life are moulded.

There are some other religions, such as Buddhism and Hinduism, that tell of incarnations and reincarnations of their founders or noted leaders. But there is always something unreal about such incarnations. something which reminds us that spirit and matter cannot be truly united. Moreover, Christianity speaks not of many incarnations but of one unique Incarnation, which sets a pattern for the Christian faith. And this Incarnation is real and vital, uniting the divine and the human in a single life.

2/JESUS OF NAZARETH, THE SON OF GOD

"Who do men say that the Son of man is?" asked Jesus of Simon on that memorable day in Caesarea Philippi. And Simon replied: "Some say John the Baptist, others say Elijah, and others Jeremiah or one of the prophets." All of these names placed Jesus in a very high category. Then Jesus asked Simon: "But who do you say that I am?" and Simon replied, "You are the Christ, the Son of the living God" (Matt. 16: 13-16). Simon believed that the only proper reply he could make to such a question was to ascribe to this man, Jesus of Nazareth, the marks of divinity. This was an amazing confession for a Jew to make, seeing that from infancy he was taught that God is one and that divinity must be ascribed to God alone.

According to the New Testament Jesus was about thirty years of age when He began His ministry. His message was that of repentance and the coming of the Kingdom. He gathered a group of disciples about Him. He did works of wonder and compassion and in less than three years, because of opposition He engendered among the religious and political authorities, He was crucified.

Such a statement about Jesus of Nazareth, however, is not only too brief to tell us Who He is; it is also deceptive in that it does not give us an accurate picture of the life of Him who dominates the Four Gospels and the New Testament generally. Think of the titles which the New Testament writers ascribe to Him: Lord, Christ (Messiah), Son of Man, Son of God, Master,

Great High Priest, the Lamb of God, and others. Nearly all of these titles have a divine significance. Moreover, they were used to describe Jesus by those who knew Him best. His disciples apparently exhausted their vocabulary in trying to find terms that would give something like an adequate description of who Jesus of Nazareth really was.

When we turn to the self-consciousness of Jesus we find something that is remarkable. He knows of no higher reference than Himself. "You have heard that it was said . . . *but* I say to you" (Matt. 5: 27, etc.). He declared, "Heaven and earth will pass away, but my words will not pass away" (Matt. 24: 35). He said that "all authority in heaven and on earth" had been given to Him (Matt. 28: 18); that it was by coming to Him that men could find rest for their souls (Matt. 11: 28); that He was the true revealer of the Father (John 14: 9); and that He was sinless (John 8: 46).

He who can speak thus is no mere prophet. Some one greater than the prophets is here. He is, as Simon confessed, the Son of God. "No man ever spoke like this man" (John 7: 46), was the comment of the Roman officer concerning Jesus. We read also that the people were "astonished at His teaching, for He taught them as one who had authority, and not as the scribes" (Mk. 1: 22). He made the blind to see, the deaf to hear, and the lame to walk. And after His crucifixion He was raised from the dead and lives in that divine Tri-unity with the Father and the Holy Spirit, ever making intercession for us. Such a person is God's incarnate Son, the God-man who is the Founder and Foundation of the gospel we proclaim to the world.

Jesus was both human and divine. Although these two aspects of his nature are inseparable, let us try to see what is involved in emphasizing the "doubleness" in this one life by looking at each aspect separately.

3 / JESUS THE MAN

Jesus was truly human. He was born, He suffered and He died. When the disciples first met Him they saw a man who attracted them. Not until they came to know Him better did they realize that He was more than man.

One of the heresies against which the early Church had to contend was "docetism," the name of which is derived from a Greek word meaning "to seem." The docetists accepted Jesus as divine but they said it was not possible for one who was divine to become human. To such people Jesus' earthly life was a phantom; it was all a matter of seeming. Jesus only seemed to be tempted, to eat, to grow weary, to suffer and to die. It was against this docetic heresy that the three General Epistles of St. John were directed. "Every spirit which confesses that Jesus Christ has come in the flesh is of God, and every spirit which does not confess Jesus (is come in the flesh) is not of God" (1 John 4: 2, 3).

There is no evidence in the Gospels to suggest that the disciples ever considered whether Jesus was truly human. The humanity was so obvious that it was taken for granted. The question whether their Lord was human would have sounded nonsensical to them. They were His friends. They talked with Him, heard Him pray, listened to His teaching, watched Him healing the sick, sat at table with Him, wandered in the fields with Him, saw Him grow weary and tired and at the last they looked at Him on a cross. To the disciples, Jesus was truly man.

There is a sense in which we can say that we do not really know what man is until we see Jesus. Manhood is largely a matter of moral and spiritual qualities which manifest themselves in attitudes and acts of love. Here the manhood of the Master is supreme. Compared with His manhood all the rest of us are lacking in perfect human qualities. And the reason for this is that we are sinners. Sin leaves the mark of imperfection on all of us. It mars our manhood. But when we are confronted with a complete break with sin, as in the person of Jesus Christ, we find that human life shines forth in all its original glory. It was this truly human aspect of Jesus' character which inspired George Matheson to write:

Son of Man, whenever I doubt of life, I think of Thee. Nothing
is so impossible as that Thou shouldst be dead. I can imagine
the hills to dissolve in vapour and the stars to melt in smoke,
and the rivers to empty themselves in sheer exhaustion; but I find
no limit in Thee. Thou never growest old to me. Last century
is old, last year is an obsolete fashion, but Thou art not obsolete.
Thou art abreast of all the centuries. I have never come up with
Thee, modern as I am.

4 / THE SIGNIFICANCE OF JESUS'   HUMAN LIFE

This emphasis on the human life of Jesus is of abiding significance for Christian belief about man and the life of man with
God. For one thing, it shows us that there is a real affinity
between God and man. There can be no ultimate separation
between the divine and the human since God came into this
world in the form of a man. We realize that our sin has created
a barrier between ourselves and God. But Christ, Who was without sin, and Who did always those things that pleased the Father,
has taken down the barrier and opened for all of us a way into
the presence of the Most High God (Eph. 2: 4). He restores the
relationship between man and God that our sin destroyed.

Moreover, this basic affinity between God and man is set
forth in the teaching that man is made in the divine image
(Gen. 1: 27). Sin defiled, blurred or blotted this image so that
it could not shine forth. But in Jesus the image is restored for
all of us. He "bears the very stamp (image)" (Heb. 1: 3) of God's
nature and in Him this image is like a burning and a shining
light. Unlike us, He is completely obedient to the Father's
will (John 8: 29). Thus he shows us the basic affinity of our
nature for God so that it is only in obedience to God that we have
true freedom.

Again, because of Jesus' truly human life we know that our
Lord understands our struggles and our cares, our trials and our
pains. "Because he himself has suffered and been tempted, he is
able to help those who are tempted" (Heb. 2: 18). "He learned
obedience through what he suffered" (Heb. 5: 8). He is touched

with a feeling of our infirmities. He knows what anguish and suffering mean from first-hand experience and in a measure few of us can comprehend. He prayed that the cup of suffering might pass from Him. How human this is! This is no Saviour aloof from us and unacquainted with our human life in this world of time. He is One Who wept over sin (Lk. 19: 41) and sorrow (John 11: 35). There is a sense in which we can call Him Saviour because He is the kinsman of all of us.

Further, the human aspect of Jesus' life also tells us that since there was a genuine incarnation the worth and significance of man to God can be seen in a new light. It was man—and not some other creature—in whom God chose to dwell. By this act God has given man a new dignity and status. Henceforth every man is a brother for whom Christ came and lived and died.

Since Jesus came man must be regarded in a new light, the light of the cross. Through the love of God in Christ crucified we see that men, for whom He died, should not be treated as slaves, robots or mere things. For in this act of self-giving on the cross Christ has wedded Himself to humanity forever. Henceforth when man suffers, Christ suffers; when man is treated unjustly, Christ suffers; when man is persecuted, Christ suffers. "As you did it to one of the least of these my brethren, you did it to me," said Jesus (Matt. 25: 40). It is before the cross that we see the depth of meaning in these words.

Further, because of the Incarnation we are challenged by the gospel we proclaim to incarnate, or embody, this gospel in human life and in our social relationships. Our love must be manifest in deed as well as in word. Since God showed forth His love in human life, we who believe in God must express God's love in the daily round and common task. "If any one says, 'I love God,' and hates his brother, he is a liar; for he who does not love his brother whom he has seen, cannot love God whom he has not seen" (1 John 4: 20). Hence the Incarnation is an incentive to Christian social action.

5 / JESUS CHRIST, THE DIVINE LORD

We next turn to a consideration of the divine aspect of the life of Jesus Christ. He Who was truly man was also God in human form. It was God, and none other, Who was incarnate in the human life of Jesus. As Athanasius pointed out in the fourth century, the one who would be man's Saviour must be truly man; but he must also be God and have divine power in order to deliver man from sin. It is such a person that we have in Jesus Christ.

Because man is made in the divine image we can say that to some degree God is incarnate in every man. The Incarnation of Jesus Christ, however, is of a different sort. We had our beginning in time. Jesus Christ existed before all time. He was the divine Lord Who came into the world, not one who came out of it. Thus the difference between Christ and ourselves is not simply a difference of degree; it is also a difference in kind. "In him the whole fulness of deity dwells bodily' (Col. 2: 9). In Jesus Christ God Himself was as fully present as it is possible for Him to be present in a human life. Jesus' thought, purpose and will were those of the Father in Heaven. In and through the words and acts and life of Jesus God came to men.

The Christian definition of God is the God and Father of our Lord Jesus Christ. "God was in Christ" (2 Cor. 5: 19). Among other things this means that we do not determine our thinking about Jesus by a prior concept we have of God. Rather, our thought of God is determined by our knowledge of Jesus Christ in whom God dwells. Because of this truth the apostolic benediction does not begin with a statement about God but with "the grace of the Lord Jesus Christ" (2 Cor. 13: 14), through Whom we know the love of God and the fellowship of the Spirit. In Jesus Christ, the man, we see

> God's presence, and His very Self,
> And essence all divine.

The distinction between the deity of the Lord Jesus Christ and man, created by God, is set forth in the Nicene Creed in the words, "begotten not made" (created). A man may make (create) a chair or a table—something quite different from himself. But a man begets sons—that which is of his own nature. So Jesus Christ is God's "only (begotten) Son," partaking of the very nature of the Father. He was not created or made. He is co-eternal with the Father. He has neither beginning nor ending.

It has been pointed out by many writers that the distinctive New Testament teaching about God is that of His fatherhood. The belief that God is Father is only one of several pictures of God in the Old Testament. But in the New Testament God's fatherhood is given particular emphasis. "Father," with or without descriptive adjectives, is Jesus' name for God. This usage shows us Jesus' awareness of His filial relationship to God. Above all, it is in and through Jesus Christ, the Son, that we come to know God as Father. "No one comes to the Father, but by me" (John 14: 6), said Jesus. The Son is the "express image" of the Father's person.

6/DOCTRINES THAT WITNESS TO CHRIST'S LORDSHIP

The most important witness in the New Testament to the Lordship of Jesus Christ is the resurrection (See chapter 4). But there are other testimonies to His Lordship such as the various names and titles by which He was known: Jesus, Christ, Lord, Son of Man, Son of God, etc.—all of which have messianic and divine significance. In addition there are several New Testament doctrines that witness to His divine Lordship. Among these we single out three for special mention:

(i) *The Virgin Birth.* (More correctly the Virgin Conception. Matt. 1: 8-25; Lk. 1: 36-38.) John S. Whale writes that "the meaning of the Virgin Birth is ultimately dogmatic: it is one of the many ways in which the New Testament asserts that the Son of God came into history; that He did not come out of it."[1]

[1]John S. Whale, *Christian Doctrine,* p. 109.

Jesus did not begin to live at a certain point in time. He came into time. He "came down from heaven and was incarnate by the Holy Ghost of the Virgin Mary." His birth of a Virgin tells us of His divine uniqueness.

Since Jesus was born of a woman like all other men, the Virgin Birth does not diminish but emphasizes the true humanity of Christ. This doctrine also reminds us that God has come to renew His creation. Christ is the second or last Adam, the inaugurator of the redeemed race. Christ is thus the miracle person, the divine Son and Lord, who entered history in a miraculous fashion and who, following His crucifixion, rose and ascended miraculously to the Father in heaven. The Virgin Birth testifies to the divine Lordship of Christ and thus to Him as a person of mystery, one whose origin is above history but who also came into history.

(ii) *The Word*. In the Prologue of the Gospel of John, Christ is described as the Word of God. "In the beginning was the Word, and the Word was with God, and the Word was God . . . and the Word was made flesh" (John 1: 1, 14).

This conception of the divine Word came from the Old Testament where the Word of God is one of the ways of speaking of God's creative activity. According to Hebrew thought, it was by the Word of God that the world was created by God. And the Prologue of the Fourth Gospel is a parallel to the early verses of Genesis.

While the concept of the Word (*logos*) was also current in Greek thought, its meaning in the Fourth Gospel is entirely Hebraic because the Word is incarnate in Christ. The Word was so embodied in Him that men had seen Him with their eyes, had heard Him speak and had handled Him with their hands (1 John 1: 1-3).

This doctrine of Christ as God's Word is one more way of stating that Jesus was the embodiment of the divine Word. He was the unique Son of God and Lord of life Who came from God and returned to reign with God in heaven.

(iii) *The Self-Emptying of Christ.* The doctrine of the self-emptying (*kenosis*) of Christ states in another way the same Christian truth that Jesus is Lord. This Jesus, says St. Paul, is one who shared a life with God the Father before all ages. He "emptied himself, that is, stripped himself of all his heavenly power and glory," taking the form of a servant, being born in the likeness of men. "And being found in human form he humbled himself and became obedient unto death, even death on a cross. Therefore God has highly exalted him" (Phil. 2: 8-9). This picture of the self-emptying of Christ, this sacrificing of His heavenly glory on our behalf, tells us plainly of the Christ Who existed before time; Who came into time at a certain point in history; and Who returned to a realm beyond time to rule with the Father.

Thus the One Who was born in Bethlehem on the first Christmas is not "of man, or from men" but God's only Son, our Lord. No wonder that Dorothy L. Sayers, commenting on the passage, "The Word became flesh and dwelt among us" (John 1: 14), exclaims: "If this is not exciting, then what in heaven's name is worthy to be called exciting!" God came among men as a man. "In many and various ways God spoke of old to our fathers by the prophets; but in these last days he has spoken to us by a Son, whom he appointed the heir of all things, through whom also he created the world. He reflects the glory of God and bears the very stamp of his nature, upholding the universe by his word of power" (Heb. 1: 1-3).

It is clear from the passage in Philippians (2: 8, 9) (and elsewhere in the New Testament) that the divine condescension by Christ was an act of His own free volition. He willed to come and redeem man because of His love for men. He experienced no natural compulsion which made Him do it. Voluntarily He limited Himself, His power and His glory, and suffered death on a cross that He might win us to God. "In this is love, not that we loved God but that he loved us and sent his Son to be the expiation for our sins" (1 John 4: 10).

The Council of Chalcedon (A.D. 451), in a famous statement from the undivided Church, gave us a creed concerning the person of Christ which serves to counteract many heresies by laying stress equally on Christ's deity and humanity. The statement reads, in part, that Christ was "truly God and the same truly man . . . to be acknowledged in two natures, without confusion, without mutation, without division, without separation." Henceforth any teaching concerning the person of Christ which stresses His humanity at the cost of overlooking the equal significance of His deity, or vice versa, must be regarded as heretical. And this statement concerning the person of Christ from Chalcedon is certainly in accord with the picture of Him that we have in the New Testament where He is depicted for us as "truly God and the same truly man."

7/THE REALITY OF THE INCARNATION

Some may ask: Could the Incarnation have been real and total? The answer of Christian theology is in the affirmative.

Dr. H. R. MacKintosh points out that "the ultimate and central reality of things is Will. Now the will of Christ as Son is one with God's will not partially, or intermittently, or by way of metaphor; it is one identically."[2] Our wills may be in harmony with, or obedient to, or parallel with, God's will but never identical with it. The redeeming Christ is viewed by Christian faith not as partially divine but as "very God of very God." And since God's nature revealed by Christ is love we see the highest manifestation of this love in the self-limitation of the Incarnation and the self-abnegation of Calvary.

Was Christ's ego, then, human or divine? "Neither and both" is our reply—and this is not double-talk. If His ego were human He would be only another man. If it were divine He would be

[2]H. R. MacKintosh, *The Doctrine of the Person of Jesus Christ*, p. 417.

remote from us and there would be no real Incarnation. But "all the relevant facts compel us to affirm that the subject of the human life of Christ is the Logos (Word), the Eternal Son, but in the form and under the conditions of human existence."[3] His human will, then, is also His divine will which is restrained from its full exercise by the conditions of His own choosing. These are not two wills but one, for the God-man is the most unified and integrated person Who ever lived.

8 / THE DECISIVE QUESTION

According to the record of the First Gospel, Jesus once asked the Pharisees the most decisive question we all have to answer: "What do you think of the Christ" (Matt. 22: 42)? It was this question that the Church Council at Nicea (A.D. 325) wrestled with, a Council at which the formula of Athanasius was accepted rather than that of Arius who claimed that Christ had been created and was, therefore, not truly God. In opposition to Arius the Council adopted the Athanasian formula that Christ was of "one substance (*homoousios*) with the Father," and that, therefore, He was truly God as well as truly man. No wonder Thomas Carlyle's comment on this decision is significant: "If Arianism had won, Christianity would have dwindled into a legend."[4] What was at stake at the Council of Nicea was nothing less than the source of man's redemption. Is our Saviour God incarnate, or someone other than God? And the Church's categorical reply in this statement from Nicea was that He was "very God of very God . . . and was made man."

If then, the claim of the Church and the heart of the gospel we proclaim is that Jesus Christ is the God-man, we must resist all attempts to dress Him up in the role of a mere religious leader, or a great teacher of morals, or a noted prophet. C. S. Lewis writes:

[3]Vincent Taylor, *The Person of Christ*, p. 289.
[4]John S. Whale, *Christian Doctrine*, p. 110 (Quoted).

A man who was merely a man and said the sort of things Jesus said wouldn't be a great moral teacher. He'd either be a lunatic—on a level with the man who says he's a poached egg— or else he'd be the devil of Hell. You must make your choice. Either this man was, and is, the Son of God: or else a mad-man or something worse. You can shut him up for a fool, you can spit on him and kill him as a demon; or you can fall at his feet and call him Lord and God. But don't let us come with any patronizing nonsense about his being a great moral teacher. He hasn't left that open to us. He didn't intend to.[5]

Moreover, if Jesus Christ is the God-man let us be done with all talk about imitating Him. How can we imitate One Who is God's "only-begotten Son"? We become sons of God by faith in Christ. He was the unique divine Son of God from all eternity.

Some one may object and say that Jesus told us to follow His example (John 13: 15). This is so. But we must remember that whenever we read in the New Testament that Jesus has given us an example, or that He is our example, the term and setting always have one reference, namely, to His spirit of service and sacrifice. In this, and this alone, we can imitate Him. But we cannot take His place as Saviour and Lord. "There is one God, and there is one Mediator between God and men, the man Christ Jesus" (1 Tim. 2: 5). Any mediating work we may do from God to men must be under the guidance, power and inspiration of Him Who is the one Mediator between heaven and earth, the man Christ Jesus.

9/LIFE MEANS CHRIST

Since Jesus Christ is God Incarnate, man must find life's meaning and purpose in and through Him. "Life means Christ to me" (Phil. 1: 21, Moffatt), wrote St. Paul. The Christian views all life "sub specie Christi," that is, "under the aspect of Christ."

Many ancient Greek thinkers, especially the Stoics, claimed that it was through the cultivation of reason (*nous*) that man

[5]C. S. Lewis, *Broadcast Talks*, p. 50f.

could find life's meaning, since we live in a rational universe. Therefore the Greeks laid great emphasis on the training of the intellect and the development of intellectual virtues.

Without depreciating in any respect the importance of reason and the intellect, Christianity went a step beyond the Greeks and said that since God is love, the meaning of life is to be found in love. Love is not simply an attribute of God; it is His very nature. And God's love has been made plain to us in Jesus Christ.

Hence the gospel we declare tells us that it is by the life of love for God and man that we discover life's purpose. "Beloved, if God so loved us, we also ought to love one another" (1 John 4: 11). Love means life and life means love. Love is the very law of life, a law which is beyond law. Love is not an elective; it is an imperative. "Thou shalt love" (Matt. 22: 37ff). "God is love and he who abides in love abides in God, and God abides in him. . . We love, because he first loved us" (1 John 4: 16, 19). And at the heart of such love is the cross of self-sacrifice.

Jesus said, "Whoever would save his life will lose it; and whoever loses his life for my sake, he will save it" (Luke 9: 24). Here in simple words we find stated the basic law of humanity. The man who lives with a grasping, self-centred spirit loses life. But the man who gives his all in love for Christ's sake finds that "life means intensely and means good."

One of the pioneer Protestant missionaries to the Indians in Western Canada in the nineteenth century was Robert Rundle, after whom Mount Rundle at Banff, Alberta, is named. Most of Rundle's life was spent ministering to the Indians in an unselfish and dedicated manner. When he died a plaque was erected to commemorate his life and work. On it the Indians printed this inscription: "He came to us poor. He left poor. He made many rich."

Jesus Christ, the incarnate Lord, came to us poor. He was born in a stable. He left poor. He was crucified on a lonely hill outside Jerusalem between two thieves. He made many rich for He saved the world.

FOR FURTHER READING

God Was in Christ, by D. M. Baillie

The Person of Christ in New Testament Teaching, by Vincent Taylor

Revelation in Christ, by William Nicholls

CHAPTER THREE

QUESTIONS FOR DISCUSSION

1 *Can you give some modern evidence of the need for reconciliation?*

2 *How can the death of Jesus more than nineteen centuries ago reconcile man to God today?*

3 *If God is good why does He not forgive us without requiring the death of Christ?*

4 *What is the attitude of the "man-in-the-street" toward sin?*

5 *Can psychiatrists replace the ministry of the Church when it comes to getting rid of guilt complexes?*

6 *How should we fight the devil?*

7 *Since suffering is inevitable in this kind of a world, should we do anything to relieve it? Why?*

8 *Isn't Christianity a long-faced, sad religion because it is forever talking about a cross? Should we not have a religion of joy instead?*

9 *How would you bring comfort to a friend who has been told that he has only a short time to live because of incurable cancer? What would you say to him about God's purpose and love?*

10 *Since God does everything in giving man salvation will we not be inclined to shun good works and take things easy? Why work at all if it does not bring us nearer the Kingdom?*

11 *Isn't this so-called need for salvation largely an emotional need? If so, will it not be met by proper home training and a good well-rounded education?*

12 *The biblical emphasis is on "believing." The modern emphasis is on "doing." Is there a basic conflict here? If so, how can these emphases be reconciled?*

Reconciliation

1 / INTRODUCTION

In *The Man Born To Be King* by Dorothy L. Sayers, the following conversation takes place between Pilate and his wife Claudia in the Governor's palace:

Pilate: Claudia, Claudia, tell me—what was this dream of yours?

Claudia: I was in a ship at sea, voyaging among the islands of the Aegean. At first the weather seemed calm and sunny—but presently, the sky darkened—and the sea began to toss with the wind. . . Then out of the east, there came a cry, strange and piercing . . .

"pan ho megas tethnéke
pan ho megas tethnéke"

and I said to the captain, "what do they cry?" And he answered—"Great Pan is dead." And I asked him, "How can God die?" And he answered, "Don't you remember? They crucified him. He suffered under Pontius Pilate." . . . Then all the people in the ship turned their faces to me and said: "Pontius Pilate" . . . he suffered under Pontius Pilate . . . in all tongues and all voices . . . even the little children with their mothers . . . your name, husband, your name continually . . . "he suffered under Pontius Pilate."[1]

[1] P. 310. Play II, Scene 2.

In this chapter we are to consider why Jesus Christ "suffered under Pontius Pilate"; why He "was crucified, dead, and buried." And one of the New Testament words which sums up this work of Christ on the cross is "reconciliation."

The term "reconcile" is a very common one in the English language, having an appropriate meaning beyond the bounds of Christianity. When two people, let us say, are "not on speaking terms," we claim they are estranged from each other. And when they become friends again we say they are "reconciled." The differences between them have been removed. The barriers to friendship are down. In a more deep and profound way, as we shall see in this chapter, Christ has removed the barriers to friendship between man and God and man and man and "has made both one" (Eph. 2: 14).

The life, teachings and deeds of Jesus on earth were manifestations or "signs" of the presence of God in Him. Then came the crucifixion. And it is the belief of the New Testament writers that in this supreme deed on the cross God was there also. "God was in Christ, reconciling the world unto himself" (2 Cor. 5: 19). Paul writes that the only thing in which he can boast is "the cross of our Lord Jesus Christ, by which the world has been crucified to me, and I to the world" (Gal. 6: 14).

The cross should not be considered as something separate from the life of Christ. The cross is the epitome, a summary in a deed, of all that Jesus did and said during His ministry. It was the Christ of Galilee, of the Mount of Transfiguration, of the Judgment Hall—the Christ whom the disciples knew so well—Who died on Calvary. So Christ's death and life are inseparable. "For if while we were enemies, we were reconciled to God by the death of his Son," writes St. Paul, "much more, now that we are reconciled, shall we be saved by his life" (Rom. 5: 10).

It is apparent in the epistles of St. Paul that reconciliation by Christ has universal significance. This is declared not only in the second chapter of Ephesians (11-21) but also in Colossians (1: 19-22). Christ came to reconcile "all things, whether in heaven or in earth, making peace by the blood of his cross"

(Col. 1: 20). Such passages help us to grasp something of the significance of Christ's reconciling work for the whole of creation.

Man needs to be reconciled to God because of the evil in his own heart and the evil in the world. Evil has two main forms. There is moral evil or wickedness, which is better described as the sin of man. Then there is the evil of pain, suffering, frustration, etc., which results from ignorance, error, "acts of God" such as earthquakes, typhoons, etc. Whatever the cause the results are evil in that they hinder man from attaining the more abundant life in this world.

We will consider separately these two main types of evil and the reconciliation which God offers to men.

2 / MAN AND HIS SIN

(i) *The Meaning of Sin*. From the Christian point of view the basic truth about human nature is that man is made "in the image of God" (Gen. 1: 27). He is created for fellowship with God. He is made to depend on God. But this creature, man, who has been created to soar to the heights of spiritual living, chooses to descend to the depths of ignominy and shame. He is a "falling" creature. He perverts the relationship between himself and God. He endeavours to live independently of God and thus he falls into sin.

Sin is an indication of the fact that man, by his disobedience, has corrupted the highest faculties of his nature, his capacity for fellowship with God. "Man's unhappiness, as I construe, comes of his greatness," wrote Thomas Carlyle, "it is because there is an Infinite in him, which with all his cunning he cannot bury under the Finite."[2] Man is both "the glory and the shame of the universe," Pascal wrote, adding, "Who is miserable but a dethroned king?" Man was made for heaven but he descends to hell. He was created for fellowship with God but he denies God and breaks this fellowship. He is "enslaved to sin" (Rom. 6: 6) and worships and serves "the creature rather than the Creator" (Rom. 1: 25).

[2]Thomas Carlyle, *Sartor Resartus*, p. 143.

When we look at man's life objectively we see, on the one hand, the truth of the psalmist's words that from the point of view of creation man is made "a little lower than God" (Ps. 8: 5). On the other hand, from the point of view of redemption, man is "sold under sin" (Rom. 7: 14). And this predicament in which man finds himself constitutes his need for being redeemed from sin and being reconciled to God.

We must distinguish between sins and sin. Sins are acts of deviation from the moral law—murder, adultery, theft, etc. These are acts or words which contradict the supreme law of love. But underneath all sins is sin; an inner attitude of mind and heart and will which rebels against God, which endeavours to escape from God. Sin is wrongness within the soul, an inner corruption of spirit and outlook. Sin is deeply personal and is like a moral cancer that feeds on the vitals of man's spiritual life. Masefield pictures Saul Kane, the rowdy poacher and brawler, who had committed many sins, coming to realize one day that there was something more basically wrong with him than these outward acts of evil; these were motivated by something evil within his soul, so he meditates on "The harm I done by being me" ("The Everlasting Mercy"). Saul Kane's "me", his ego, was sinful.

St. Paul sometimes thinks of sin as quasi-personal (e.g., Rom. 7: 20). Sin is "this body of death" (Rom. 7: 24), and the wages it pays is death (Rom. 6: 23). Sin separates man from man (Eph. 2: 14) and man from God (Eph. 2: 12). Sin lies at the root of all sins, not least of all "man's inhumanity to man" and his repudiation of God. Dr. Carl Jung, the noted psychologist, says that man's besetting problem is his "godalmightiness," his attempt to displace God. And this is sin. "Thou hast not yet considered the gravity of sin," wrote Archbishop Anselm. And neither has modern man, insofar as its seriousness is concerned. For sin is not merely "missing the mark," or falling away from a standard. Sin is coming short of God's glory, a wilful failure to have fellowship with God. Sin is turning one's back on God, insulting the Almighty, repudiating divine love. Sin is following the devices and desires of our own hearts instead of obeying the divine voice.

The Bible tells us "that all have sinned and fall short of the glory of God" (Rom. 3: 23). Such a statement reminds us not only that sin is universal but also that the term "sin" is a religious one. It has no meaning apart from man's relationship to his Maker.

(ii) *Sin as Estrangement.* Paul Tillich describes man's condition as "the state of estrangement. Man is estranged from the ground of his being, from other beings, and from himself."[3] Estrangement is "the basic characteristic of man's predicament." According to Tillich, this estrangement can be seen as unbelief, or lack of trust in God, disrupting the essential unity between man and God. It can also be regarded as *hubris,* a Greek word meaning self-elevation, pride, or that state of assumed greatness through which man tries to dethrone God. And again estrangement may be looked upon as "concupiscence," a term much wider in meaning than sexual lust because it refers to all desires, whether for power or fame or wealth, and to such desires as hunger and sex, which come between man and God.

(iii) *The Consequences of Sin.* These consequences are many and varied. Besides alienation between man and God, man and man, and man and his true self, there is that corruption "that hardens a' within," that perversion of one's sense of values, a gradual turning to a love of evil, with distress and confusion at every turn, personally and socially. And over all is God's condemnation, since "the face of the Lord is against evil-doers" (Ps. 34: 16). The goodness of God and the evil in man are at enmity with each other. God is "of purer eyes than to behold (countenance or approve) evil and (cannot) look on wrong" (Hab. 1: 13). And the prophet calls upon evil men to "remove the evil" of their "doings from before" God's eyes (Is. 1: 16).

But it is just at this point that man feels his frustration most keenly. He feels helpless and hopeless. He cannot deliver himself from the evil within him or the acts of evil he commits. He is

[3] Paul Tillich, *Systematic Theology,* Vol. 2, p. 44.

"lost and undone." "Woe is me," is man's cry as he confronts the sin in his heart.

St. Paul describes our human predicament, our sense of failure and guilt and helplessness. "Wretched man that I am! Who will deliver me from this body of death" (Rom. 7: 24)? We can all appreciate the anguish which lies back of these words. Man knows that he needs salvation from sin, reconciliation with God. But he cannot save himself. Who will deliver him? Who will come and save him?

(iv) *The Good News of the Gospel.* It is when man faces his predicament caused by sin that he realizes that the Christian gospel has good news to offer all men. God has come to deliver man from the guilt and power of sin. For the great Christian affirmation is that in the presence of sin man can exultantly cry, "Thanks be to God through Jesus Christ our Lord" (Rom. 7: 25). Through faith in Jesus Christ man can enter into a saving experience of God's forgiveness; he can be "ransomed, healed, restored, forgiven"; he can be born again from above. This is all the doing of the Lord and it is marvellous in our eyes.

"Therefore, since we are justified by faith, we have peace with God through our Lord Jesus Christ. Through him we have obtained access to this grace in which we stand and we rejoice in our hope of sharing the glory of God" (Rom. 5: 1, 2). This verse, according to Dr. A. M. Hunter,[4] shows us, along with other passages in St. Paul's writings, that Christian salvation has three aspects: past, present, and future. We are saved; we are being saved; and we will be saved. God in Christ has done something for man that does not have to be repeated. There is what has been called "the finished work of Christ." Christ does not have to return to earth and die again on a cross. That cross on Calvary has "once for all" opened up to us the redemptive power of the love of God. Thus we are saved. But we are also being saved because God in Christ is "working in us now" to bring us to salvation. He does not leave us to depend on a past historical

[4] A. M. Hunter, *Introducing New Testament Theology*, p. 91.

act but, through the power of His Spirit, he works in our lives and in the Church to make this love shown on Calvary a present reality. But the fulness of Christ's salvation is not yet realized. "We do not yet see everything in subjection to him" (Heb. 2: 8). Therefore, we live in expectation and anticipation of His coming in glory "to unite all things in" Christ (Eph. 1: 10). Then we shall be saved and His Kingdom will be established for ever and ever.

Paul Tillich states: "If I were asked to sum up the Christian message for our time in two words, I would say with Paul: It is the message of a 'New Creation'."[5] "If anyone is in Christ," writes the Apostle, "he is a new creation; the old has passed away, behold, the new has come" (2 Cor. 5: 17). Newness of life through Christ—this is the positive side of reconciliation. God's reconciling power in Christ delivers us from sin and death to the life that is abundant and eternal.

Reconciliation is then, an act of God in Christ whereby man is delivered from a condition of estrangement and alienation to one of fellowship and communion with God. Through this reconciliation man is the recipient of God's gracious favour. God is the subject and man is the object in the work of reconciliation. And the result is the establishing of a new personal relationship of trust and love between man and God, man and man, and man and his true self. "All this is from God, who through Christ reconciled us to Himself and gave us the ministry of reconciliation" (2 Cor. 5: 17).

(v) *The Means of Reconciliation*. The means God used to reconcile man to God was the self-sacrifice of Christ on the cross. The cross portrays for us in a deed the truth that "God so loved the world that He gave His only Son, that whoever believes in him should not perish but have eternal life. For God sent the Son into the world, not to condemn the world, but that the world might be saved through him" (John 3: 16, 17). Thus the cross has become the central symbol of the Christian faith. For that

[5]Paul Tillich, *The New Being*, p. 15.

cross on Calvary tells us not only of "the lamb of God, who takes away the sin of the world" (John 1: 29) but also of a deeper truth that there was a lamb slain "from the foundation of the world" (Rev. 13: 8). Calvary's cross has, so to speak, drawn aside the curtain which hid the face of God and lets us see, for one brief moment of time, the reconciling, redemptive, loving heart of the Father.

Various theories have been offered concerning reconciliation or atonement. Some say that "Jesus died to satisfy divine justice." This is not the sort of language we would use today, but originally the sentence had a profound meaning. "Divine justice" is the justice of love and "to satisfy" refers to the perfect obedience which God demands of man and which man, by his sin, could not give. Such perfect obedience has been given for us by Christ: "Not as I will, but as thou wilt" (Matt. 26: 39). Still others speak of Christ as being our "substitute". Sometimes this theory is set forth in language that we find offensive or difficult. But here again let us think of Christ's substitution in terms of love. Have not our parents often taken our place, suffered for us and even in our stead; that is, "substituted" for us? How much more has our Saviour, Who "was wounded for our transgressions" and "bruised for our iniquities" (Is. 53: 5), taken our place. He died for sin that was not His own.

Some Old Testament scholars have pointed out that this passage in Isaiah to which we have just referred (chapter 53), which is one of the Suffering Servant passages of the Old Testament, has its true meaning brought to light in the death of Christ on the cross. He was the perfect Suffering Servant. Moreover, we are told that the element of substitution is an integral part of the Suffering Servant concept because Isaiah 53 tells us of God's Servant bearing the sin of others in a vicarious manner, that is, suffering for others out of His great love for them.[6]

What we must realize is that Christ's act of reconciliation is much more important than our theories concerning this act. The

[6]See *The Expositor's Bible*, Commentary on Isaiah (53) by Sir George Adam Smith.

deed is God's deed which saves. The theories are man's interpretation of this deed. Because we are thinking beings we must
have our theories, and their place is not to be minimized. But
let us get our perspective right: the deed is more significant than
our interpretation of it.

In relation to our sin, Christ on His cross does two things.
First He condemns our sin. We see this in the fact of human
guilt. The conscience of man tells him that he is responsible for
his wrong-doing and, even more, his wrong-being. Why is it,
for example, that an ancient drama like *Oedipus Rex* by
Sophocles should maintain such a strong appeal to men over the
centuries? You recall that this story tells how the son of the King
and Queen of Thebes was removed from his parents at birth and
how later, when he had grown to manhood, he unwittingly slew
his father and married his mother. When at length he discovered
the awesome truth, his sense of guilt was so overwhelming that
he put out his own eyes and condemned himself to exile. The
reason for the persistent attraction of this story, introduced into
modern psychology by Freud, is that man is still face to face with
the problem of guilt. Guilt haunts man and plays havoc with
his peace of mind. And unless it is taken away, as modern
psychology and psychiatry as well as religion will testify, the
consequences will be tragic indeed. The "stuff'd bosom" must
be cleansed, as Macbeth told the physician concerning his wife,
"of that perilous stuff which weighs upon the heart."

In the second place, the Christ on His cross forgives our sin.
Our guilt is taken away and our sin is purged by His love. "If
we say we have no sin, we deceive ourselves, and the truth is not
in us. If we confess our sins, he is faithful and just, and will
forgive our sins and cleanse us from all unrighteousness" (1 John
1: 8, 9).

The cross reminds us that Christ forgives the penitent sinner
at a great cost. We have been "bought with a price" (1 Cor. 6: 20).
We have been saved at the cost of His blood—an image from the
history of religious sacrifice which reminds us how costly our
salvation is (See Rom. 3: 25; 5: 9; Eph. 1: 17; Col. 1: 14). In

war and in peace many people have "shed their blood" for the sake of others and their freedom. For the "blood is the life" (Lev. 17: 11, etc.). It refers to the utmost in sacrifice and self-giving for others. And if the blood of animals purified the flesh, "how much more," then, "shall the blood of Christ, who through the eternal Spirit offered himself without blemish to God, purify your conscience from dead works to serve the living God" (Heb. 9: 14).

From the cross Jesus prayed, "Father, forgive them; for they know not what they do" (Luke 23: 34). And the New Testament always interprets God's love in terms of the cross and its forgiveness. "By this we know love, that he laid down his life for us" (1 John 3: 16). "In this is love, not that we loved God but that he loved us and sent his son to be the expiation for our sins" (1 John 4: 10). "He died that we might be forgiven"—the just for the unjust. "Greater love has no man than this, that a man lay down his life for his friends" (John 15: 12). Jesus laid down His life also for His enemies. "God shows His love for us in that while we were yet sinners Christ died for us" (Rom. 5: 8).

> O love of God! O sin of man!
> In this dread act your strength is tried
> And victory remains with love:
> Jesus, Our Lord, is crucified.

3 / THE PROBLEM OF EVIL

Six million Jews were killed by Hitler and his legions but "God said never a word." A promising young life is taken and a scoundrel lives to an old age. A Christ is crucified at thirty-three and a cheat and liar like Annas lives beyond the span of three score years and ten. "My God, my God, why?" How can we justify the ways of God to man? This is the heart of the problem of evil.

(i) *Some Aspects of the Problem.* The problem of evil is greatly aggravated by the Christian gospel's declaration that God is love. If God is not good the problem of pain is still acute but we are not perplexed by trying to understand the why of it. But when we say that God is love the problem of evil in a world created and sustained by such a God becomes almost overwhelming.

There are, however, some aspects of this problem that ought to be clear to us. For instance, the sin of man causes countless thousands to mourn. Because of selfishness and greed millions of people have not sufficient of this world's goods. Power-loving people ride roughshod over the interests of many.

Then, too, man suffers from the sins of former generations. The solidarity of the race in evil as well as in goodness is an obvious fact of history. What, for instance, was the originating cause of the Second World War? Hitler? The Versailles Treaty? Undoubtedly these were contributing factors leading to this War. But the originating causes of the Second World War lie far back in history, in nineteenth century politics and European culture, in the lust for power of certain groups in many generations who have bequeathed to us an evil inheritance. This is one aspect of the tremendous truth in the misnamed doctrine of "original sin". Original sin is hereditary sin not in the biological but in the social sense. The doctrine teaches the solidarity of all men in sin or, as Paul would say, "in Adam," the representative of our fallen race.

Again, we can see that some suffering comes because of man's ignorance. Some of this suffering disappears when man is educated and enlightened (*e.g.*, as modern medicine has met the problem of disease). The development of modern technology, for instance, has enabled men to build dams on large rivers where previously destructive floods took a toll in lives, food and shelter.

Some suffering has arisen because man is a free being. God gave man the dread gift of free will. But this meant that man could say "No" as well as "Yes" to his Creator. God does not coerce man into doing what is good, else the deed would not be man's moral choice. Only in freedom can man be held morally responsible. But man has used this freedom in a manner that opposes God's moral order. He has permitted slums to be erected. lives to be blighted, souls to be damned from birth by social conditions which are contrary to God's order. Such an irresponsible use of free will had led to suffering for the innocent as well as for the guilty. But we cannot have it otherwise in the kind of world in which we live (See James 4: 1, 2).

(ii) *The Devil.* Some people would say that the cause of evil in the world is the power and the work of the devil.

We have no desire to discard the concept of the devil. His satanic majesty laughs with glee at those who are thus deceived. Who or what the devil is we cannot tell. He is "the prince of darkness" and we ought not to expect to have much light on him or his ways. The moment we think we have the devil cornered we can be sure it is not he, for he will turn up in some other place or way. The fact is that there are powers of evil in our world which deceive us, militate against our best desires, frustrate our purposes, and sometimes turn this world into a hell for many people. Whatever may be the source of these powers outside of human life and our human inheritance, there is no reason why we should not ascribe them to the devil.

But placing the blame for evil on the devil does not solve the problem. It only pushes the problem back one stage further. Why the devil? Why does a good God permit him to exist and carry on his nefarious work?

Two things we must remember respecting biblical teaching and the work of the devil. First, the devil is not God's opposite number, with power equal to that of God. There is not going on between God and the devil a seesaw fight of which the final outcome is in doubt. God is the Lord. Even the devil is subject to Him and can only exist by His permission. Paul refers to the devil as sending forth "the man of lawlessness" and "the son of perdition" "who opposes and exalts himself against every so-called god or object of worship, so that he takes his seat in the temple of God, proclaiming himself to be God. . . And you know what is restraining him now so that he may be revealed in his time.

For the mystery of lawlessness is already at work; only he who now restrains it will do so until he is out of the way. And then the lawless one will be revealed, and the Lord Jesus will slay him with the breath of his mouth and destroy him by his appearing and his coming" (2 Thess. 2: 3-9). "The coming of the lawless one by the activity of Satan," states St. Paul, in effect, must not blind our eyes to the deeper truth that he is still subject to God and will be ultimately destroyed at the coming of Christ Who will gather all things to Himself.

The second thing the Bible would tell us about our relationship to the devil is that we cannot place the responsibility on the devil for our sins. It is we, not the devil alone, who must give an account of the deeds done in the body. It is we who must stand before the judgment seat of Christ. We are the people who have sinned, and we are responsible for our sin.

(iii) *The Suffering of the Righteous.* But the heart of the problem still remains. If God is both good and almighty, why do the righteous suffer? This is the problem faced by the writer of the book of Job. In ancient times it was believed that suffering was a sign of one's sinfulness, while prosperity was an indication of one's righteousness. The book of Job refutes such a theory and the crucifixion of Jesus denies it utterly. For on this theory Jesus was the greatest sinner who ever lived. The teaching of Jesus also contradicts this pagan doctrine that virtue is rewarded with prosperity (See Luke 13: 1-5).

The book of Job (*e.g.* chapter 37) points out that we do not know all that is involved in the purpose of God and the working out of His purpose in the world. His ordering of the universe is too great for our finite minds to fathom. His ways are past finding out. Therefore a certain measure of humility and awe should characterize the attitude of those who would try to find a complete solution of the problem of evil in our world.

Moreover, when we deal with this problem from the standpoint of God let us bear in mind that He has made his world law-abiding. At 32 degrees—not 40 or 50 degrees—water freezes. So when the thermometer drops to 20 degrees below zero and people are outdoors in such weather with insufficient clothing on their bodies they will freeze to death. That is an evil—but it is the result of living without regard to the weather conditions of the world in which God has placed us. What a topsy-turvy world this would be if one day water froze at 32 degrees and the next day at 42 degrees. In spite of the apparent evil which sometimes comes from the reign of law we would not change this sort of world, even if we could. We wish to live in a universe that is dependable.

When we say that we live in a law-abiding universe we do not mean to imply that the world is static. In the material world the atom is of central importance and the structure of the atom, as the modern physicist informs us, is dynamic. Nor must we forget that in this world the supreme law under God is the law of personality. God acts, through the will of men, though not exclusively so. Personality is the most important factor in the world and the personality of God has freedom to act in His creation as He wills, though always in conformity with the laws of His own nature.

All of these statements do not "solve" the problem of the suffering of the righteous but at least they help us to understand a little better some of the reasons why the innocent as well as the guilty experience pain. But the final word of the Christian gospel on this problem is the word of the cross.

(iv) *The Cross and Suffering.* God is love. And the one Who manifested this love supremely was Jesus Christ. He showed us God's love not in spite of suffering but in and through the suffering of the cross. Jesus did not permit the fact of pain to blot out the Father's presence. His last word from the cross was, "Father, into thy hands I commit my spirit" (Luke 23: 46). God's love now is seen to be sacrificial, suffering love.

In this kind of a world when sin meets goodness there is always a crucifixion. When human wickedness encounters the spirit of unselfishness someone is done to death. The reason for this is that God's love is moral and He will not stoop to immoral means and force people to obey Him. His method is always one of moral persuasion, not of coercion or compulsion.

When we think of God as love let us take from our minds all thoughts of some sentimental creature who always seeks to do what is pleasing to us. C. S. Lewis says that some people think of God as "a grandfather in heaven—a senile benevolence, who, as they say, 'liked to see young people enjoying themselves' and whose plan for the universe was simply that it might be truly said at the end of each day, 'a good time was had by all'."[7] This is not the picture of God the Father revealed to us by His Son on the cross.

God's purpose for man, in the light of which we should view all pain, is not that we should have a "good time" but that we should develop characters that are suitable for fellowship with Him. This means discipline, self-sacrifice, and a willingness to endure. Like our Lord, we must be made perfect through suffering. There is no other way. The way of the cross leads home to character, to perfection, and to God. Thus the cross instead of denying God's love by its suffering becomes, in the Christian alchemy, the means by which God's love can be made manifest before the world.

Having said all this about suffering both from the human and the divine side, inasmuch as we are able to bring some light to bear on this problem, we must realize that a "surd" factor, an "unknown element", still remains. We must beware of "over-explaining" the problem by our explanations. For there are times, such as in the presence of sorrow, when we must bow in humility before the working of God's Providence and acknowledge that life has its baffling mysteries. The message of trusting in God, such as we find in Job and even more in our Lord on Calvary, will be a boon to our souls on such occasions. For even as there is mystery about the cross, with its light and its darkness, so there is mystery about this problem of human suffering.

But our gospel takes us a step further—and it is a momentous

[7] C. S. Lewis, *The Problem of Pain*, p. 28.

step. It tells us that by means of the cross we, with Christ, can
be victorious over all evil. The victory remains with His
sacrificial love. So while the gospel does not offer us a theoretical
solution of the problem of evil it does something better; it offers
us a triumphant faith. It gives us a power with which to overcome evil, to fight the devil, and to use suffering for God's glory.
It grants us a strength with which we can endure pain and thus
take captivity captive. Like Wordsworth's Happy Warrior, the
Christian can "turn his necessity to glorious gain." "For whatever
is born of God overcomes the world; and this is the victory that
overcomes the world, our faith" (1 John 5: 4). This faith is faith
in Christ crucified Who by His triumph over death on the first
Easter vanquished pain and evil.

Christianity will not let us explain away the fact of evil. It
tells us plainly that we have a foe and that we have a tough fight
on our hands. But thank God, we also have a victory through
Christ who has reconciled all things — even pain and evil and
suffering — to Himself. So as we stand before "the giant agony
of the world," or as we confront the fact of sin and evil, guilt
and anguish, we also know that God always causes us to triumph
in Christ Jesus. "Who shall separate us from the love of Christ?"
asks St. Paul. "Shall tribulation, or distress, or persecution, or
famine, or nakedness, or peril, or sword? . . . No, in all these
things we are more than conquerors through him who loved us.
For I am sure that neither death, nor life, nor angels, nor prin-
cipalities, nor things present, nor things to come, nor powers,
nor height, nor depth, nor anything else in all creation, will be
able to separate us from the love of God in Christ Jesus our
Lord" (Rom. 8: 35, 37-39). This is the final Christian answer to
the problem of evil and it is an answer that is given only through
faith in Jesus Christ.

4 / DEBTORS TO DIVINE GRACE

The task of rescuing man from sin and evil and reconciling
him to God is spoken of as a work of grace. "You know the grace

of our Lord Jesus Christ, that though he was rich, yet for your sakes he became poor, so that by his poverty you might become rich" (2 Cor. 8: 9).

It has been said that there are basically only two kinds of religion: one is that in which man tries to put God in his debt and the other is that in which man acknowledges his indebtedness to God. The first is a religion of works. The second is a religion of grace. And the Christian gospel is founded on the grace of our Lord Jesus Christ.

Norman Snaith[8] reminds us that "the idea of grace more than any other idea binds the two testaments together into a complete whole, for the Bible is the story of the saving work of God, that is, of the grace of God." Grace tells us of God's favour toward us—unmerited and free to all who live by faith in Christ. Grace is God's love in action for sinful men, reaching out to man in his lost condition and rescuing man from the sin that so easily besets him. And so the watchword of the Protestant Reformation was "By grace you have been saved through faith; and this is not your own doing, it is the gift of God" (Eph. 2: 8). Here is the good news of the gospel. God is so gracious that He has come to deliver us, even in our unworthiness.

We may recall the words that Francis Thompson penned in "The Hound of Heaven." God is speaking:

> 'Strange, piteous, futile thing! . . .
> How little worthy of any love thou art!
> Whom wilt thou find to love ignoble thee,
> Save Me, save only Me?'[9]

God "does not deal with us according to our sins, nor requite us according to our iniquities. For as the heavens are high above the earth, so great is his steadfast love toward those who fear him; as far as the east is from the west, so far does he remove our transgressions from us" (Ps. 103: 10-12).

God in Christ does not deal with sinners on a basis of their

[8]*A Theological Word Book of the Bible*, edited by A. Richardson. Article "Grace" by Norman Snaith, p. 101.
[9]Francis Thompson, *Complete Poems*, Modern Library, p. 93.

just deserts. If He did so, our case before Him would be hopeless. But God comes to us in His grace, with a loving-kindness and a tender mercy far beyond our deserts.

John Baillie in *Invitation to Pilgrimage* tells a story related by C. H. Spurgeon about one of his fellow ministers who went to the house of a poor old woman with a contribution of money for the payment of the rent. "He knocked again and again, but failed to get any response. Nevertheless, the old woman was all the time within, and her explanation afterwards was, 'I heard the knocking, but I thought it was the man come to ask for the rent'."[10]

How often we mistake God like that! We think that He comes with demands. He first comes to us with gifts, the greatest of which is the gift of His reconciling grace. It is ours for the taking—by faith.

To many people the gospel seems too good to be true. They cannot think that God can be so generous—which is an indication of how circumscribed is their own generosity. You may recall that Wordsworth wrote a sonnet, "Inside of King's College Chapel, Cambridge," in which he described "this immense and glorious work." Could it be that love was too lavish on this occasion? Was it not wasteful to erect such a costly structure? No!

> Give all thou canst! High Heaven rejects the lore
> Of nicely-calculated less or more. . .

The cross tells us that God has rejected the "nicely-calculated less or more." Christ gave His all for you and for me, even when we were unworthy of it. This is grace. And grace makes us debtors to God. We sing, "Nothing in my hand I bring, Simply to Thy cross I cling." This hymn reminds us that we owe everything to God—our life and our salvation. We have nothing in ourselves whereof we can boast: our only boast can be in the cross of our Lord Jesus Christ.

In Dorothy L. Sayers' play, *The Zeal of Thy House,* the central figure is William of Sens, the architect and craftsman of

---

[10]P. 48.

Canterbury Cathedral. As the work progressed, William became filled with self-confidence. The praise of men ministered to his pride. Later, through suffering and personal disappointment, he became a transformed person. Near the end of the drama we find William, now a subdued and humble soul, saying:

> To all of you, I owe a debt of love
> Which I will pay with love. Only to God,
> That royal creditor, no debt remains.
> He from the treasure of His great heart hath paid
> The whole sum due, and cancelled out the bond.

The cross raised on Calvary's hill testifies to the grace of God which "has cancelled out the bond." "Thanks be to God, who gives us the victory through our Lord Jesus Christ" (1 Cor. 15: 57).

5 / THE CALL TO SERVICE

"Beloved, if God so loved us, we also ought to love one another" (1 John 4: 11). This is always the motive for service in the New Testament. We must give because God gave in Christ. We must serve because Christ took a basin and towel and washed the disciples' feet, leaving us an example of humble and lowly service for others (John 13: 5f.). Out of gratitude for a mercy so undeserved, out of thankfulness for a grace so freely bestowed, we must go forth to sacrifice and to give, even as Christ gave His life a ransom for many. If the gracious, reconciling love of God in Christ crucified does not constrain a man to give himself and give and give again, even until he has spent all, then we do not know what will move him to service and to sacrifice. But the testimony of many is like that of Father George Tyrrell who, when tempted to give up the struggle of reforming his Church, declared, "The figure of that strange man on His cross always sends me back to my work again." So may it be until time shall end!

After the execution of Montrose, according to a story by Margaret Irwin, his betrothed entered a nunnery and took vows. In spite of many unsavoury stories about her, she became in time an abbess. Years later her sister asked her bluntly, "Why did you take vows?" and she answered: "Because the story of the God Who gave up His Godhead and His human life for the world of humans has always moved me, not with sorrow or pity, but with exaltation. Could anything be more glorious than to have so much to give and to give it all?" Such is the constraint that comes to many from "that strange man on His cross."

FOR FURTHER READING

A Plain Man Looks at the Cross, by Leslie D. Weatherhead

The Problem of Pain, by C. S. Lewis

CHAPTER FOUR

QUESTIONS FOR DISCUSSION

1 *What would you single out as the most important evidence for the resurrection of Jesus Christ?*

2 *How do we know that Christ's tomb was empty on that First Easter?*

3 *Was it not misleading for St. Paul to write about "the resurrection of the body" when he did not mean the physical body (1 Cor. 15)?*

4 *What are our reasons for believing in life after death?*

5 *Communism teaches that to lead people to believe in life after death is a way of distracting their attention from social injustices here and now. What do you think?*

6 *Isn't it enough to follow Jesus in our earthly life and forget about the life to come?*

7 *Should we not teach people to concentrate on life — not death?*

8 *Was St. Paul correct in connecting belief in the life hereafter with one's duties in the present (1 Cor. 15: 58)?*

9 *Isn't the Oriental picture of Christ as an all-powerful king out of date in a world in which we are stressing a democratic form of government?*

10 *Why do you think Protestants have very little to say about priests and their place in religion?*

11 *How can we tell when a true prophet appears in the Church?*

12 *Since we no longer believe in a flat earth with heaven "above" it, should we not discard belief in the ascension of Christ?*

CHAPTER FOUR

Resurrection

1 / THE SIGNIFICANCE OF THE RESURRECTION

A friend of mine owns a book, bound in fine leather, which has this title: *The Life and Morals of Jesus of Nazareth*. Its author is none other than Thomas Jefferson. The book consists of clippings from the four Gospels which are sayings and acts of Jesus selected from these Gospels by Jefferson, who was a rationalist. Anything in the large number of sayings and acts of Jesus in the Gospels that did not conform to his beliefs Jefferson omitted. He did a sort of pasting job, based on his own rationalistic presuppositions. And the book ends with this sentence from St. Matthew's Gospel: "And he rolled a great stone to the door of the sepulchre, and departed" (Matt. 27: 60).

What a caricature of the real gospel, which tells us that a stone rolled to the door of His sepulchre was not the end of Jesus of Nazareth but rather that the stone was rolled away from the door of the sepulchre and that an angel announced, "He is not here; for He has risen" (Matt. 28: 6). Apart from this message of the risen Lord the "life and morals of Jesus of Nazareth" would be no more valuable than an account of the life and

59

morals of Socrates or Confucius. It is the resurrection of Jesus Christ from the dead that gives the Church a gospel to proclaim.

There are several events and teachings recorded in the New Testament which witness to the Lordship of Jesus Christ. But all such events and teachings are of secondary importance in comparison with the teaching of His resurrection. In fact all doctrines which witness to Christ's Lordship are dependent doctrines because they would not be sufficient in themselves to establish His Lordship. But Christ's resurrection is the supreme New Testament evidence of His divine Sonship. This is the miracle of miracles. St. Paul considers the resurrection to be the chief manifestation of God's almighty power, for he refers to "the working of his (God's) great might, which he accomplished in Christ when he raised him from the dead" (Eph. 1: 19, 20). Peter, in his sermon at Pentecost, ended with this stirring proclamation that "this Jesus God raised up, and of that we are all witnesses . . . let all the house of Israel therefore know assuredly that God hath made him both Lord and Christ, this Jesus whom you crucified" (Acts 2: 32, 36). Christ is declared to be the Son of God by His resurrection from the grave. Therefore it is in the good news of the resurrection that we find the ultimate testimony of the New Testament writers to the Lordship of Christ. He must be Lord because death could not hold Him.

The resurrection also has tremendous significance for the life of the Church. More than one writer has pointed out that the missionary expansion of the Church is itself a splendid witness to Christ's resurrection. What changed the despairing, fleeing disciples of that dark Friday when Jesus was crucified into flaming apostles who went everywhere proclaiming the Word of life? It was the resurrection. We have a brief survey of the story of the early Church in the Book of Acts in which we see also the burden of Christian preaching which is "Jesus and the resurrection" (e.g. Acts 4: 3; 17: 18). It was the resurrection which gave impetus and motivation to the evangelistic zeal of the Church. The Christians now had a gospel of life to offer to men.

2 / THE NEW TESTAMENT WITNESS TO THE RESURRECTION

All four Gospels tell us that Jesus rose from the grave (Matt. 28; Mark 16; Luke 24; John 20, 21). It is true that there are discrepancies and differences in the accounts of what really happened on that first Easter; but this is no more than one should expect when we consider that different people are giving their own personal account of this amazing story. In fact, these differences in the accounts of the resurrection testify to the authenticity of the story rather than against it. All the writers tell us that Jesus, Who was crucified, came again and appeared to His disciples. There is also no doubt from these narratives that Jesus Himself believed during His earthly ministry that He would rise again. How often He referred to His resurrection on "the third day," "after three days" (*e.g.* Mark 8: 31; 9: 31; 10: 34). He expected His cause to be vindicated and the Kingdom to come "in power" by His triumph over death (*e.g.* Matt. 16: 21; Luke 18: 33). And we have noted previously how prominent is the message of the resurrection in the book of Acts.

When we turn to the New Testament Epistles we also find that they are based on the unquestioned belief that Jesus rose again. St. Paul declares that Jesus Christ was "designated Son of God in power according to the Spirit of holiness by his resurrection from the dead" (Rom. 1: 4; see also 1 John 5: 11; 1 Peter 1: 3; Heb. 8: 1; Rev. 1: 5, etc.). In fact, it is belief in Christ's resurrection which made possible the writings of the New Testament. Without this "mightiest of all the mighty acts of God" it is impossible to conceive how or why the New Testament should have been written. It is not so much the New Testament that explains the resurrection; it is the resurrection that explains the New Testament, even as it explains the Church which produced the New Testament.

We can see the altogether overwhelming importance of Christ's resurrection in the Christian evangel if we turn to one of the earliest books in the New Testament—First Corinthians. In chapter 15 St. Paul declares that he is only stating what the

Church has passed on to him, what is common belief among the Christians, namely "that Christ died for our sins in accordance with the scriptures, that he was buried, that he was raised on the third day in accordance with the scriptures, and that he appeared to Cephas, then to the twelve" (vs. 3-5). Later in this chapter St. Paul points out that certain things must inevitably follow "if Christ has not been raised" (v. 14). These things are: (i) Christian preaching is in vain; that is, it is empty of content. You have no good news to declare since Christ was crucified, dead and buried — and that's the end of Him. (ii) the faith of a Christian and of the Church is in vain for the simple reason that it has nothing substantial, triumphant and abiding on which to build. The best you can say, then, is that a good man died for his beliefs. Too bad! But so did Socrates and countless others. Your faith has no rootage in an event which could turn your sunsets into sunrises. (iii) If Christ has not been raised you are misrepresenting God, because your gospel is that God raised Him up when He really did nothing of the sort. You are putting God in a bad light. (iv) If Christ has not been raised you are "still in your sins." There is no forgiveness and new life available through a dead Christ. (v) And there is no hope for any of us beyond the grave (v. 18). Then we are of all men "most to be pitied." The future for men without an immortal hope is dark indeed. In fact what the Apostle is telling us here is that apart from Christ's resurrection we have no gospel at all to proclaim to the world.

After painting such a bleak outlook of the kind of world in which we live if Christ has not been raised, St. Paul comes forth with a ringing affirmation which casts aside all doubt. "But in fact Christ has been raised from the dead, the first fruits of those who have fallen asleep" (1 Cor. 15: 20). No words of ours in the twentieth century can over-emphasize the central New Testament witness in the first century that the Church's gospel was a gospel of a risen Lord.

Moreover, Christ's resurrection on the first day of the week was at the heart of the Church's worship, for the early Christians changed their stated day of worship from the Jewish Sabbath (Saturday) to "the Lord's Day" (Sunday), the first day of the week. Thus each Lord's Day when we gather together for corporate worship we do so in the faith that Jesus is alive forevermore (See Acts 20: 7; 1 Cor. 16: 2; Rev. 1: 10).

3 / THE RESURRECTION OF THE BODY

When St. Paul preached at Athens (Acts 17: 16-32) he had a sceptical audience. They watched to hear what this "babbler" (literally "seed-picker") would have to say, what new ideas on religion he had to offer, what new opinions in philosophy he was ready to expound. For the Athenians religion consisted largely in playing around with new ideas about God and man and destiny, a sort of intellectual pastime, but they did not get down to real religious living. So the Athenians listened for a time. But when St. Paul came to the end of his discourse and said that God had raised Jesus from the dead, we are told that "some mocked", while others said, "We will hear you again about this," and a few believed.

One reason for the scepticism of some of St. Paul's hearers at Athens, as well as at Corinth (1 Cor. 15), was that Greek philosophy contained many ideas about belief in immortality, or the immortality of the soul, though it was a type of immortality that was not really personal. Socrates believed in it. Plato taught it. Some have even thought that in this matter of life after death Greek philosophy was a schoolmaster to lead us to Christ.

But this is far from the truth. The Greek belief in the immortality of the soul was, to begin with, a big guess. Moreover, in content it was very different from the Christian belief in life after death which is stated in terms of the resurrection of the body. Greek ideas of life hereafter were based on a dualism between body and soul. The body, being material, was inherently evil; the soul, being naturally good, was inherently suited to live on in some semi-personal, ghost-like existence, minus a body.

The body was the prison house of the soul and so it should be shed as soon as possible. Plato believed that by the contemplation of philosophy in this world, and the refinement of the mind, one already began to discard the body which obscured the shining forth of true ideas in the soul. The way to immortality, said the Greeks, was to find release from the body.

Both at Athens and Corinth St. Paul had some hearers who already believed in the immortality of the soul after the fashion of Plato and the Greeks. Hence, when St. Paul came preaching a bodily life hereafter, which they had been taught to despise, they were baffled. "But some will say, 'How are the dead raised? With what kind of body do they come?'" (1 Cor. 15: 35). He makes it very plain (1 Cor. 15: 50) that he is not talking about a physical body of flesh and blood which cannot inherit the kingdom, because this body is perishable. He claims that there are various kinds of bodies—bodies created to suit different spheres of existence. But all such bodies are given by God. And, he says, what God gives us through Christ is an imperishable, spiritual body, suited to the world of the spirit.

In other words, St. Paul is stating that the resurrection of Christians after death has some likeness to the resurrection of Christ from the grave, and that was a bodily resurrection. And the reason why St. Paul is stressing the body so strongly is that he wishes to emphasize the truth that personality lives on. The body is the personal principle of identity. Moreover, while there is a likeness between Christ's resurrection and ours there is also unlikeness, because He is the Christ of God and we are sinful men relying on grace to grant us eternal life. But Christ's resurrection is the first-fruits, the certain promise, of life to come for those who abide in Him. And that certitude of Christian faith is based on the reality of the empty tomb. Death could not hold Christ. His physical body, by the power of God Who raised Him, was transformed in some miraculous manner into a spiritual body. It was a body with many similarities to His earthly body because He could be recognized; but it was a glorified body, unlike his earthly body because, for example, He could enter when "the doors were shut" (John 20: 26).

There is nothing with which we can compare the resurrection of Christ. It is unique, as His person is unique. The One who rose from the grave was the incomparable one.

In the language of St. Paul and in that of the Apostles' Creed the resurrection of the body stands for the resurrection of the whole man. We do not go to God as disembodied spirits, impersonal "somethings." We go to God fully personal, with all those powers which are necessary for personal life. Thus the doctrine of the resurrection of the body tells us that our historical, earthly life is not something worthless to God, but something which is of such value in God's eyes that He transforms it, "takes it up" into a heavenly sphere, a spiritual state of existence where our personality, once clothed in physical form, is now embodied in a spiritual form; not "unclothed," as St. Paul says, but further clothed (2 Cor. 5: 4).

And when we apply the doctrine of the resurrection of the body to the corporate company of believers, the Church, we can understand that the life to come is corporate. The Church is Christ's body, the community of His redeemed. They praise Him night and day in His temple. And this makes clear to us the communal life of those who live with Him, such a life as to rule out all narrow, individualistic concepts of salvation as unfit for the Kingdom.

4 / THE CONSEQUENCES OF THE RESURRECTION

Because we believe in the resurrection of Christ certain things follow:

(a) *Tragedy is turned into triumph.* There can be no denial of the fact that apart from the Easter faith, Good Friday would have been a very dark day indeed for the disciples of Jesus. But the light of life which God brought forth from the grave on the first Easter transformed the apparent tragedy of the cross into triumph. Since that first Easter Christians have known that it was not in spite of, but by means of, the cross that Christ gained the victory over sin and death. That is why Protestants usually represent the cross as empty, and not as a crucifix, though the latter is not without meaning. By an empty cross we depict the truth that Christ rose again out of death and he must, therefore, not be considered as a martyr who died for his cause—and nothing more.

So great has been this triumph of Christ that the world has never been the same since the first Easter. Now we know that sacrificial love, such as Jesus manifested in His life and death, can never be destroyed. Now we know that love is stronger than hate; that truth is greater than falsehood.

> Right forever on the scaffold,
> Wrong forever on the throne.

No! The Easter faith tells us that wrong has been defeated and that death lies dead. Sin, in principle, has been vanquished and the devil and his angels will finally be cast into the bottomless pit forever. The resurrection makes clear in any event that He "must reign until he has put all his enemies under his feet" (1 Cor. 15: 25).

Let us refer again to St. Paul's sermon at Athens (Acts 17). When he mentioned Jesus and His resurrection from the dead it was within the context of announcing to this sophisticated audience, to whom morality was a very relative affair, that God would judge the world in righteousness by this man, Jesus Christ. For, to St. Paul's thinking, it was Christ's resurrection which supplied authentic proof that there is a final moral judge, that the world is based on moral foundations, that righteousness has now been vindicated, that God's eternal order stands forever sure against the assaults of the devil. The resurrection of Christ, therefore, "is not just a personal survival; it is a cosmic victory."[1] That is, it has a relevance to the whole creation. No wonder,

[1]James S. Stewart, A Faith to Proclaim, p. 122.

then, that St. Paul could write about "the rulers of this age, who are doomed to pass away" (1 Cor. 2: 6). They rule now, but the signature of death is upon them because Christ has risen. No rule or authority can ultimately prevail against His power.

(b) *The new age has begun.* In the Old Testament men looked forward to "the coming age," the "day of the Lord," the arrival of the Messiah to establish His Kingdom. Now, said the Christians, He is here. We know this is the "coming One" because He has risen from the grave. All the promises of God "find their Yes in Him" (2 Cor. 1: 20). A new dispensation, the age of the New Covenant, has arrived. The Golden Age about which men have dreamed has begun. "The time is fulfilled, and the kingdom of God is at hand; repent, and believe the gospel" (Mark 1: 15). Christ's resurrection underscored the truth of His own words.

In this new age inaugurated by the resurrection believers have a firm basis for faith and hope. These qualities are no longer dependent on men's attitudes and virtues. Faith has its centre in One who turned the worst into the best and transformed death into victory. Faith henceforth is not merely some subjective experience which has no objective ground. Faith is now rooted in One Who has ushered in the new day of God, Who Himself has stood the test of the world's evil and has come off more than conqueror. The Christian's faith is faith in Him Who has conquered all. "This is the victory that overcomes the world, our faith" (1 John 5: 4).

Hope also has a new ground and centre for the Christian. The term "hope" is always used in the singular in the New Testament because it has only one reference — Jesus Christ. Hope is not based on human aspirations or wishes. It is definitely united to Him Who has begotten us "anew to a living hope through the resurrection of Jesus Christ from the dead, and to an inheritance which is imperishable, undefiled, and unfading, reserved in heaven for you" (1 Peter 1: 2,3). The Christian's hope is based on what has already happened. Because of the resurrection he is sure that certain other things will happen in the future.

(c) *Death has been vanquished.* Because Christ lives we shall live also. "I am the resurrection and the life," said Jesus, "he who believes in me, though he die, yet shall he live, and whoever lives and believes in me shall never die" (John 11: 25, 26).

There is no adequate philosophy of life that does not include a philosophy of death. There is a real sense in which life is a meditation on death. Unless we have something to say to ourselves and others as we face the fact of our mortality we have little to say that is worthwhile about other matters. "As for man, his days are as grass; he flourishes like a flower of the field; for the wind passes over it, and it is gone, and its place knows it no more" (Ps. 103: 15, 16). The Bible, with its realistic appraisal of our human situation, makes us face the fact of death. Are we, then, to build for tomorrow on the foundation of "unyielding despair?"

A conversation once took place between an old saint, and a young, ambitious lad. "What are you going to do with your life?" asked the old man. "I will learn my trade," replied the lad. "And then?" asked the old gentleman. "I will set up my business," said the lad. "And then?" "I will make my fortune." "And then?" "I suppose I shall grow old and retire and live on my money." "And then?" "I suppose that some day I will die." "And then?" There was no reply. The lad had not yet considered death.

When we come to contemplate the last "And then?" we must remember that our future is entirely in the hands of God. We must rely on His mercy and renew our hope through the resurrection of Christ Who has opened for us the gates of life eternal. He has conquered death for all of us. "Death is swallowed up in victory. O death where is thy victory? O death where is thy sting? The sting of death is sin, and the power of sin is the law. But thanks be to God, who gives us the victory through our Lord Jesus Christ" (1 Cor. 15: 54-56).

This implies, of course, that man cannot rely on anything in himself if he is to cherish an immortal hope. He cannot earn or merit or achieve the life of the world to come with God. His only confidence is in the grace of the Lord Jesus Christ Who gives to all who believe in Him the gift of new life hereafter as well as here. He looks to Christ Who has brought life and immortality to light through His gospel. He trusts in Him Who has said, "Let not your hearts be troubled; believe in God, believe also in me. In my father's house are many rooms; if it were not so, would I have told you that I go to prepare a place for you?" (John 14: 1,2). So Christians "remember Jesus Christ, risen from the dead" (2 Tim. 2: 8).

5 / THE CHALLENGE OF THE RESURRECTION

"If you then have been raised with Christ, seek the things that are above," writes St. Paul, "where Christ is, seated at the right hand of God. Set your mind on things that are above, not on things that are on the earth. For you have died, and your life is hid with Christ in God" (Col. 3: 1-4). In these lines the apostle is not writing of a state or condition beyond the grave. The death he writes about is being dead unto sin through Christ's forgiveness. What the apostle is really doing in these words is to show to Christians the challenge which comes to their everyday living because Christ has been raised. "Because you believe in Christ's resurrection," St. Paul seems to say, "your manner of life must be thus and so." It must be a life consistent with belief in Christ, the living Lord.

Belief in the resurrection is not "pie in the sky when you die." It gives vitality to the life that now is. Belief in the life beyond through Christ becomes the inspiration of the life that we live on earth. Now we know, with the certitude of faith, that "there will never be one lost good"; that all the values for which we strive and the Kingdom to which we belong shall have no end. The temptation to become a "tired rebel" fades out of one's life when he knows he can work with patience because he realizes he can "leave now for dogs and apes" since "man has forever."

Listen again to St. Paul. He has given a long and sustained argument, ending with a note of affirmation in the life to come because Christ has won the victory through His resurrection. Then follows: "therefore"—that is because of this faith which St. Paul has been expounding regarding our hope through the risen Christ — "therefore, my beloved brethren, be steadfast, immovable, always abounding in the work of the Lord, knowing that in the Lord your labour is not in vain" (1 Cor. 15: 58). He is saying, in effect, that we should realize that because Christ is risen our work for Christ does not add up to zero in the end. Now we can work with renewed zeal, with steadfastness and perseverance, because we are assured by the resurrection that the final word is not death but life in Christ, the Christ Who said to the seer on Patmos, "Fear not, I am the first and the last, and the living one; I died, and behold I am alive for evermore, and I have the key of Death and Hades" (Rev. 1: 17, 18).

The Church of our day will find new vision and vitality where the Church of former times found it: through faith in Christ's resurrection and the challenge this faith presents. A salutation of the Christians in the Roman Empire was "The Lord is risen," to which the reply was made, "He is risen indeed!" If we really believe this truth, that is, believe it with all our heart and soul and mind and strength, we shall discover that there will come to the Church a new release of spiritual life and a new zest to undertake the tasks of His Kingdom. "If you have heard the Easter message," writes Karl Barth, "you can no longer run around with a tragic face and lead the humourless existence of a man who has no hope."[2]

Only the God Who raised up Jesus Christ from the grave can raise up the Church from lethargy and faithlessness to serve Him. It is this revolutionary faith which is contained in this benediction: "Now may the God of peace who brought again from the dead our Lord Jesus, the great shepherd of the sheep, by the blood of the eternal covenant, equip you with everything good

[2]Karl Barth, *Dogmatics in Outline*, p. 123.

that you may do his will, working in you that which is pleasing in his sight, through Jesus Christ; to whom be glory for ever and ever. Amen" (Heb. 13: 20, 21).

6 / THE ASCENSION

For a period of about forty days following the first Easter Christ made appearances to His disciples (Matt. 28: 9-20; Luke 24: 50-53; John 20: 13; 21: 25; 1 Cor. 15: 5-8, etc.). He came among them and He withdrew from them in some mysterious manner. Then He made a final appearance which has been called "the ascension." The Apostles' Creed states it thus: "He ascended into heaven, and sitteth on the right hand of God the Father Almighty." Thus we can think of the resurrection and the ascension as two episodes of the one process in the risen life of our Lord Jesus Christ.

The setting or picture of the ascension is given in terms of Ptolemaic astronomy (Acts 1: 9-11) in which heaven was thought to be "above" the earth, which was believed to be flat. But the very manner in which the New Testament writers present the ascended Christ as now present with God the Father, whose reign was not exercised in any "place," shows us that literalism and the ascension have nothing in common. God reigns everywhere and so does the ascended Christ.

The ascension is often referred to in the New Testament (Acts 2: 33; 5: 31; Eph. 1: 20; Heb. 1: 3; 10: 12; John 20: 17, etc.) We can best think of it as an "enacted symbol" or doctrine which contains significant truth respecting our ever-living Lord.

During the forty days following His resurrection, when Christ made several appearances to His disciples, His existence was a sort of "interim" existence. He was interpreting one world to the other. But now the ascension, the last of such appearances, assures us that the pre-existent Christ, who tabernacled among men as a man for a period of time, has now resumed His former state of existence with the Father. All this is portrayed for us in earthly imagery, such as a cloud taking Him up out of the sight of the disciples (Acts 1: 9), the cloud in scripture connoting the spiritual fact of the presence of God. And while imagery is necessary in order to convey religious reality, it is what is conveyed and not the imagery that is important.

Many writers point out that there are three theological truths in the doctrine of the ascension of Christ.

(a) Christ is King. He sits "on the right hand of God the Father." This is the place of privilege, favour and authority. He exercises His reign as One Who is co-eternal with the Father. He participates in God's sovereign rule over all things. In the doctrine of the ascension we have a vindication of the truth of Jesus' statement, "All authority in heaven and on earth has been given to me" (Matt. 28: 18).

(b) He is priest. This truth is stressed in the epistle to the Hebrews (7: 25; 9: 24, etc.) though not there alone (See Eph. 2: 18; 1 Peter 3: 18). As priest, reigning in glory, He ever lives to make intercession for us. We are not forgotten in heaven. "God with man is on the throne." He is our representative before the Father, ever pleading our cause. It is through Him that we have access (Rom. 5: 2) to God. By His ascension to the right hand of the Father He has opened for us a way into the very presence of the Most High.

(c) He is prophet. He is God's supreme prophet, uttering forth God's message, taking the apostolic gospel to man (e.g. Matt. 21: 11; John 6: 14). And it is through Him, crucified, risen and ascended, that the gift of prophecy is bestowed on the Church.

At our Lord's ascension there was "no sadness of farewell." It was necessary that Christ should leave His disciples, even in the "interim" state in which He appeared during the forty days following the resurrection, the localization of His appearances severely restricted His influence over men. Thus it was "expedient" that He should depart from them that He might return to them in the Spirit and be with His people forever in every part of the earth. At the ascension Christ left His disciples in Galilee in order to be present with His Church in all times and in all places by means of the Father's gift through Him of the Holy Spirit, the "Counsellor," Who would impart to God's children the truth of "the things of Christ."

FOR FURTHER READING

The Resurrection of Christ, by J. M. Shaw

The Resurrection of Christ, by A. M. Ramsey

Did Jesus Rise from the Dead?, by James Martin

CHAPTER FIVE

QUESTIONS FOR DISCUSSION

1 *What evidence would you submit to show that the Holy Spirit is at work in the Church?*

2 *Would it be better, or worse, for our faith if we ceased to believe in the doctrine of the Trinity? Why?*

3 *What is the difference between the fellowship of the Church and the fellowship of the Boy Scouts or Rotary Club?*

4 *Would it be possible for the Church to experience another Pentecost?*

5 *What do we mean when we call the Church "the Body of Christ"?*

6 *Must we be "worthy" to unite with the Church on profession of faith?*

7 *Since the churches are so divided is it not rather unrealistic to talk about the present unity or oneness of the Church?*

8 *Why are so many Christians today not missionary-minded?*

9 *How does worship influence your thought and work and recreation?*

10 *Isn't preaching a back number in these days when nearly everyone can read, when we have television, radio and so many other forms of communication?*

11 *In difficult and dark days Martin Luther would say to himself, "I am baptized," and find new strength to carry on. Why?*

12 *"The spiritual life of the Church in our time is superficial." How can the Church recover the dimension of depth in its spiritual life?*

Communion

1 / INTRODUCTION

Our study of the gospel thus far has enabled us to see briefly that the Christian evangel centres in God's revelation in Christ, His Incarnate Son, Who came to earth, lived and taught and died on a cross in order to reconcile man to God. Then came the miracle of the first Easter with its message of life and hope through the risen Christ Who appeared on several occasions to His disciples and friends and finally ascended to the right hand of the Father in heaven.

But the gospel does not end with Christ enthroned. The drama of salvation tells us further that while Christ left His people visibly He returned to them in the power of the Spirit and that through this power He continues His saving work in the world.

2 / THE NATURE AND WORK OF THE HOLY SPIRIT

Who is the Holy Spirit? We read of His coming in the second chapter of Acts and all the epistles in the New Testament testify to His power in the early Church.

The Holy Spirit is God in action, especially among the believers. He is God coming to us and working on our minds and hearts in such a manner as to vitalize our faith and bring us into communion with God. It is the Holy Spirit Who unites Christians with Christ and with each other, for since His nature is love, unity is the very essence of His presence. It is the Holy Spirit Who makes God's forgiveness in Christ real to us and gives us the freedom of the children of God. It is the Holy Spirit Who opens to us the mystery of Christ's revelation, Who instructs us in righteousness and Who quickens our minds and hearts in the things of Christ.

When we open the Bible we read that the Spirit was present at creation's dawn. And all through the Old Testament we learn of the Spirit's activity in many situations. When we turn to the New Testament we find the Spirit present at Jesus' conception, at His baptism, when He preached His first sermon in Nazareth and on many other occasions during His ministry. Yet we also know that Jesus promised the Holy Spirit (John 16: 7) to His disciples to guide them into the truth after He would depart from them. Since the Spirit was active in the world and among God's people before Pentecost how can we speak of Him as "coming" at Pentecost?

"When the day of Pentecost had come, they were all together in one place" (Acts 2: 1). Then the Spirit came upon them suddenly and with converting power. There was an uprush of released emotions, a new joy in the hearts of the believers, and a new sense of urgency to proclaim the good news that Jesus is Lord. The Holy Spirit Who came at Pentecost was not a different Spirit from that which is found in the Old Testament and during the life and ministry of Jesus. He is the same Spirit more fully revealed, more perfectly known because of Christ and more completely apprehended. But this experience of the Holy Spirit at Pentecost was so revolutionary that by comparison with all that had gone before of the Spirit's working, this seemed something very new. And it was. But the difference was in the hearts of the disciples—a greater receptivity to the Spirit's advent, partly because of their religious experience, and also because of a better understanding of the Spirit's nature through Christ's revelation and His promise of the Spirit's coming. The latter created a sense of expectancy among the faithful.

The Holy Spirit is Christ's "alter ego." Jesus departed from His little group of followers that through the presence of the Spirit He would be with them and their spiritual descendents forever. He left one small country on earth that through the Spirit's power He could speak to men and women in all countries and in all ages. The Spirit's activity makes Christ our eternal contemporary.

3 / THE TRINITY

We have seen previously that the Christian revelation leads us to speak of God the Father and God the Son. And in this chapter we have come to speak of God the Holy Spirit. Thus we are led to believe in the triune nature of God: "God in three persons, blessed Trinity."

This belief in the Trinity arose out of the religious faith of the early Church. The doctrine of the Trinity was first a revelation of the triune God to the hearts of the believers. The first disciples were Jews—strict monotheists. They learned from Jesus that the Creator in whom they had believed was also their Father. But they also came to see that Jesus Himself was the promised Messiah, the Christ of God. They had to find a place for Jesus Christ somewhere within the Godhead. Because of their experience of redemption through Him nothing less than "the highest place that heaven affords" would be suitable for their estimate of Him. Then came Pentecost. This was still another manifestation of God — different, but the same God as known already in the Father and the Son. How were they to explain this revelation of God to themselves and to others?

Happily they came to believe in the triune nature of God (e.g., 2 Cor. 13: 14). There is no thought-out doctrine of the Trinity in the New Testament but there is the basis of this doctrine in the life and faith of the Church. It is belief in God as triune in His nature that saved the Church from polytheism. "The Bible speaks of one God, and of one God only," writes John S. Whale. "It speaks of Him in three distinct ways which are normative for Christian thinking."[1] This doctrine of the Trinity, therefore, is not the product of an arid scholasticism. It is an expression of the truth about God's nature which proceeds from the data of revelation. God has revealed Himself in a trinitarian form. We know God as Father in the Son through the Holy Spirit. As the Declaration of Savoy (1658) stated: "the doctrine of the Trinity is the foundation of all our communion with God, and comfortable dependence upon Him."[2]

When we try to understand the doctrine of the Trinity we must put out of our minds any arithmetical ideas concerning it, such as one plus one plus one equals three. This is tritheism. It is along other lines that we must proceed for analogies, or likenesses, such as the idea of an organism or body: eye, hand and foot belong to one organism and yet they are different. They belong to one centre of consciousness, yet their functions are not the same. Or we can think of Augustine's social analogy of the Trinity: God the Father is the lover; Christ the Son is the beloved; and the Holy Spirit is the love that unites them. Or, with Miss Dorothy L. Sayers,[3] we may think of the Trinity in terms of a man writing a book, at different stages: at one stage the book is an idea in the author's mind, at another it is energy being expended in writing, and at a third stage it is the printed book. All three are one and one is three. We can distinguish the "persons" but we cannot divide the "substance." Or again, with Karl Barth, we may think of God in three modes of His being, though such an analogy may lead one into the old heresy of Modalism (trinitarian teaching which does not really posit three "persons" in the Godhead). At best, analogies can lead us only a certain distance in our understanding of the doctrine of the Trinity. Here again we are face to face with a mystery of

---

[1] John S. Whale, *Christian Doctrine*, p. 114.
[2] A. M. Hunter, *Introducing New Testament Theology*, p. 119 (Quoted).
[3] *The Mind of the Maker*. See chapters 1, 2 and 3.

truth. We have some light regarding the Godhead, but we are baffled by its light and the effulgence of God's glory. Like Augustine, we speak about the Trinity not because we understand all about it but because we cannot remain silent.

We should note that the word "person" does not mean an individual, a separate entity, when we think of the persons of the Trinity. Our English word "person" comes from the Latin, *persona,* which denotes a mask. By wearing different masks one actor could play various roles in a drama. Thus the persons of the Trinity remind us that the being of God is not that of an abstract, unsocial individual. God is both personal and loving. Moreover, even those like Athanasius, Augustine, Calvin and others who have thought much about the doctrine of the Trinity, have retained the term "persons" with respect to the Trinity, not because they found it to be an adequate description of the nature of the Godhead but because any alternative presented them with sub-personal or impersonal ideas about God.

But while there are difficulties concerning the doctrine of the Trinity we realize that it sets forth the wealth of being in God's nature. Our God is not some bare, monistic Deity. He is the living, loving God – Father, Son and Holy Spirit; Creator, Redeemer and Sanctifier—whose mercy and truth are beyond the comprehension of our finite minds but whose Reality becomes clear to us in the communion of the Church and in the worship of Almighty God. As in much else in Christianity, it is in worship that we come to see the meaning and the significance of the doctrine of the Trinity.

4 / THE FELLOWSHIP OF THE SPIRIT

The Church is the fellowship of the Holy Spirit. As we read the Acts of the Apostles, which is a brief record of the life and work of the early Church, we are struck by the fact that the acts of the Church were the acts of the Holy Spirit in the Church guiding, directing and empowering the faithful in their witness for Christ.

According to the New Testament to be "in Christ" is to be
in His Church. The early Christians knew nothing of a narrow,
individualistic type of discipleship. The words addressed by a
friend to the young John Wesley, which the latter remembered
with profit all his days, well describe the spirit of primitive
Christianity: "Sir, you wish to serve God and go to heaven?
Remember that you cannot serve Him alone. You must therefore
find companions or make them; the Bible knows nothing of
solitary religion."

The descriptive word concerning the Church in the New
Testament is that it is a fellowship (*koinonia*). The root meaning
of the Greek word is "sharing." The Christian fellowship is
two-dimensional. There is fellowship with God and fellowship
among the believers. The origin of this fellowship is not in man
but in the working of the Spirit among men. This is brought out
clearly in the New Testament word for Church (*ecclesia*), which
is the Greek translation of the Hebrew term *qahal,* "the usual
term for Israel as the gathered people of God,"[4] those who are
called out of the world to serve God in the world. By the use of
this term the early Christians declared that they believed themselves to be the true people of God, called into existence by God
Who alone was the author and sustainer of the fellowship through
the Spirit. As A. M. Hunter writes: "Round the supper table
that night (in the Upper Room), the twelve sat as the nucleus
of the new Israel."[5]

The Head of the Church is the Lord Jesus Christ. Confession
of His Lordship was the badge of entrance into the Church. It
was "into this Name" of Jesus that members were baptized and
"in this Name" they continued in the fellowship. When they
broke bread together at His Table they remembered that He
was present as their unseen Host.

In the material world in which we live the Church must have
visible form. Institutions are necessary for the carrying on of
Christ's work. But it is the fellowship of the Church that is

[4]A. M. Hunter, *op. cit.,* p. 78.
[5]*Ibid.,* p. 36.

subject; it is the institution of the Church that is predicate. The fellowship lasts on, though the institution changes to meet varying needs. And at the heart of the fellowship is the Holy Spirit linking the faithful in communion with God. Institutions by and of themselves tend to become rigid, impersonal and even idolatrous. But if we think of the Church as primarily a fellowship of the Spirit which has institutions for its service to men we shall keep a right attitude toward the Church of the living God.

The nature of the fellowship is characterized by love. "By this all men will know that you are my disciples, if you have love for one another" (John 13: 35). And the kind of love Jesus has in mind is not far to seek. "This is my commandment, that you love one another *as I have loved you*" (John 15: 12). Love of the brethren that involves sharing with them and sacrificing for them is the distinguishing mark of the Christian fellowship. "See how these Christians love one another" was the testimony of an ancient pagan writer concerning life in the early Church. "Ecclesiastical ought to mean brotherly," wrote Dean Inge, and a thousand pities that it has not always been so.

5 / THE CHURCH AND PENTECOST

Pentecost is sometimes referred to as the "birthday of the Church." There is a truth in this statement if we remember that every birth is preceded by a period of gestation. And the record of the Church in the Book of Acts, following Pentecost, and in the Epistles, informs us that after Pentecost the Holy Spirit is the corporate possession of the Body of Christ and not of a few individuals. Each Church member finds the Spirit's reality within the company of believers. The Spirit's activity continues to be intensely personal. But it is in unity and fellowship that the Spirit's power and presence is to be found.

Pentecost helped the Church to believe in a more intimate manner in the old truth that God is not the God of the dead but the God of the living. The Spirit revitalized the Church and made the believers recognize the power of faith in the living God

Whom Christ had revealed to them. Now since Pentecost they knew in their hearts that He had not ceased to reveal His truth for the Spirit was indeed leading them into all truth and helping them to expound the truth to the world. God did not leave His Church people as orphans. Pentecost and the continuing presence of the Spirit with the Church served to remind the faithful in all times that God was with them to the end of the age. Therefore all is well.

6 / THE MARKS OF THE CHURCH

"I believe one Holy Catholic and Apostolic Church" is an affirmation of faith from the Nicene Creed. In this statement we have set forth the four marks of the Christian Church.

(i) *Unity.* The Church is one. Christ is one and the Church, His Body, must therefore also be one. From the point of view of the world the Church is divided. Denominationalism hinders the true manifestation of the Church's unity. But in and through the various churches there is one Church, known only to God, sustained by Christ through the Spirit and binding into one fellowship all those who believe in the Saviour. This unity is not of man's contriving. It is the gift of Christ.

There is a paradox about this matter of the unity of the Church in the New Testament. In His High Priestly prayer (John 17) Christ prays for the unity of His Church (vs. 21, 23), as if He realized that the party spirit would cause rifts in the fellowship. Moreover, St. Paul had to upbraid the Church in Corinth for the spirit of schism found in it (1 Cor. 3: 3). And while the Epistle to the Ephesians affirms the unity of God's people (2: 14, etc.) the writer also implies that unity is still something to be attained (4: 13). This serves to remind us that while unity is Christ's gift to His Church it is also something which the Church must endeavour to make known to the world more perfectly than in its present divided state.

Certainly the spirit of schism is the antithesis of true church-

manship. The party spirit in church life is a scandal. "It ought
to be horrible to us to speak or think of any fellow-Christian as
'not in communion with us'," said William Temple in the
opening sermon of the Edinburgh Conference on Faith and
Order, 1937.[6] But he also went on to say that such a meeting
as that which the representatives of the various denominations
were attending on that occasion showed that basically there was
a unity in the Church. "We could not seek union if we did not
already possess unity. Those who have nothing in common do
not deplore their estrangement. It is because we are one in our
allegiance to one Lord that we seek and hope for the way of
manifesting that unity in our witness to Him before the world."[7]
Therefore the challenge that comes to the Church from God
Himself is, "Become what you are."

(ii) *Holiness.* The Church is holy. The root meaning of the
word "holy" is "separated for the service of God." And the
Church is the people of God, the saints (holy people), who are
separated from the world by His call to serve Him in the world.
Moreover, the term "holy" is connected by derivation with such
other English words as health and wholeness, so that to speak
of the Church as holy also means that we are referring to its
wholeness through Christ.

The fact that holiness has a moral connotation today may lead
some people to think that we believe the Church consists of a
group of specially pious folk who have forsaken the world. Some
sects have interpreted holiness in this way. Of course the Church
must always have a moral challenge from a moral God to present
to her members. But any holiness or goodness in the Church is
not of men or from men. The holiness of the Church comes from
God. The Church is holy because it is indwelt by the Holy Spirit.
"The Church is holy," writes Ralph Sockman, "not because of
the goodness of her members but because of the godliness of her
begetting."[8] "The Church is not a society of integrated person-

[6]Report of the Second World Conference on Faith and Order, Edinburgh, 1937, p. 19.
[7]*Ibid.*, p. 21.
[8]Ralph W. Sockman, *How To Believe*, p. 153.

alities," writes Dr. C. C. Morrison (think of the twelve disciples), "nor of philosophers, nor of mystics, not even of good people. It is a society of broken personalities, of men and women with troubled minds, of people who know they are not good. The Christian Church is a society of sinners. It is the only society in the world, membership in which is based upon the single qualification that the candidate shall be unworthy of membership."

(iii) *Catholicity*. The Church is catholic. The word originally meant universal. It has also come to mean that the Church is "orthodox" in the sense of holding to the true faith once delivered to the saints. The term is, therefore, the antithesis of anything schismatic or partial or heretical in Christianity.

The catholicity of the Church has become more manifest in recent years through the growth of the ecumenical movement. This new and wider fellowship of believers has enabled the Church to transcend many barriers which heretofore kept them apart. The centre of this movement is in the World Council of Churches.

(iv) *Apostolicity*. The Church is apostolic. There are some who maintain that apostolicity implies an unbroken order of ministerial succession through the episcopate, a succession which dates back to the apostles. Others affirm that while succession is of value it is not of the being of the Church in the sense that without the historic episcopate there can be no Church.

The Reformed Church generally holds to a succession of presbyters within the Church as witnessing to its apostolicity. Hence the significance of the order of the Church's Ministry, with its priestly and prophetic powers, testifying to the continuity of worship and doctrine in Christ, the chief apostle (Heb. 3: 1). But even more, this Church declares that apostolicity is to be found where there is an apostolic witness to the Lord Jesus Christ. Without this witness there can be no apostolic Church, no matter how ancient and revered is its Church order. The true apostolic Church is to be found where the Word of God is preached and heard and the sacraments administered according to God's holy ordinances. It is the preaching of the apostolic gospel, recorded in the scriptures, which determines whether or not there is apostolicity in the Church.

Further, the word apostolic is a missionary word. It means that the Church is sent by Christ on a mission to the world. We have been chosen by Him and endowed by His Spirit to bring forth fruit unto His Name and to testify to "the unsearchable riches of Christ" (Eph. 3: 8).

So important is this missionary interpretation of apostolicity that Bishop Newbigin of the Church of South India writes: "We must say bluntly that when the Church ceases to be a mission, then she ceases to have any right to the titles by which she is endowed in the New Testament."[9] The besetting sin of so many Church people, that of turning the Church into an idol, an absolute, an end in itself can only be counteracted by an emphasis on her responsibility under Christ for evangelizing the world and her reliance on the Holy Spirit for the carrying out of this task. "No claim to be the Church, no historical continuity, no unbroken tradition, no apostolic succession, no theological orthodoxy, no ecclesiastical unity, no political power, no liturgical pageantry," writes Dr. John A. MacKay, "can be a substitute for the Church's missionary consecration in the form of a servant, to the redemptive purpose of God in Christ."[10]

In a time such as the present, when there is a spiritual vacuum in the heart of man and the evidence mounts each day to prove man's need to be redeemed, the Church is called by God to go forth endowed with the Spirit to proclaim the apostolic message, with apostolic zeal, to the end that man may be brought from darkness to light and the Name of God be glorified in the earth.

7 / THE MEANS OF GRACE

If the Holy Spirit is to minister to the faithful the grace of the Lord Jesus Christ, He must have channels or means by which

[9] L. J. Newbigin, *The Household of God*, p. 163.
[10] *Theology Today*, April, 1958, p. 32.

this grace can be mediated to men. And while we do not wish to restrict or confine the Spirit's activity, seeing that He can use whatever means He wills in His divine freedom, nevertheless the Church has stressed the following means of grace as of paramount importance in conveying to men the grace of Christ.

(i) *Worship.* Worship is man's response to God's gracious favour toward us. It is the context in which all other means of grace find their sustenance and the framework of the total life of a Christian. As he worships, so he serves.

Worship is essentially the response of the Church. When a Christian studies his Bible at home, or kneels in prayer at his bedside, he does so as a member of the fellowship and as one who is part of that corporate company of believers who sing God's praise and hallow His name.

Worship is prompted by the Holy Spirit. The Spirit ever makes us aware of the grace that has redeemed us. And since worship constitutes man's thankful response to God for all His benefits, man must offer the whole of himself and all that he has to God in adoration, praise and love. "I appeal to you, therefore, brethren," writes St. Paul, "by the mercies of God, to present your bodies as a living sacrifice, holy and acceptable unto God, which is your spiritual worship" (Rom. 12: 1).

(ii) *Preaching and the Sacraments.* The preaching of the Word is the showing forth of the gospel in words. In Christian preaching some portion or portions of the scripture is expounded in the light of Christ's revelation. The offer of redemption to all who come to Him by faith is heralded forth as a matter of life or death. By means of such preaching the saints are confirmed in the faith, the wayward are won back to the Kingdom, the doubters have new light cast upon their minds, the weary are given strength, the sinful find forgiveness and the lost are brought home to the flock. Even as Jesus came preaching, so the Church must continue to publish abroad the glad tidings that Christ has redeemed the world.

Within the Reformed faith the preaching of the Word has

been united with the administration of the sacraments. "The preached Word of the gospel comes to its own climax in the visible Word of the Eucharist. Similarly, the Eucharist presupposes the preached Word of the gospel; it is the sacred pledge and seal of the promises of God."[11] This is why in so many churches the open Bible on the pulpit and the Holy Table in front of the pulpit form the focus in Protestant worship.

For preaching and the administration of the two sacraments we have dominical (that is, from our Lord) authority. Christ instituted all three means of grace and commanded His Church to continue them. They are the channels through which the Holy Spirit takes of the things of Christ and makes them real to us so that we are nourished in the faith.

We speak of the sacraments as symbols, but symbols are more than merely pictures or metaphors. The ancient meaning of the term "symbol" is a coming together, a meeting, or in this instance an encounter between God and man. What the sacraments symbolize is God coming to man in a gracious manner. Hence there are no "empty" or "bare" sacraments, for sacraments become, through the Spirit's action, means by which God conveys to men His saving grace.

It is God Who acts in the sacraments. In preaching we hear God's Word. In the sacraments we see His deed. In both preaching and the sacraments the same God conveys the same grace. Therefore man's part in the sacraments is secondary. Man receives from God, the Giver of every good and perfect gift.

In the sacraments we see a reenactment of the Incarnation, the spiritual and the material being conjoined to bring to man the reality of God. And by continuing to relate these sacraments to the Word of the incarnate Lord we save them on the one hand from superstition, and on the other from mere memorialism.

(iii) *Baptism.* Baptism is the sign of entrance into Christ's Church. By means of Baptism the child (or adult) is admitted into the fellowship of the redeemed. Here God's cleansing grace is to be found. Within this realm of redemption the baptized

[11]John S. Whale, *Christian Doctrine*, p. 154.

person finds that which is necessary for his own growth in grace as well as the power which renews the Church in faith.

Since Christ's promise is to all who believe, together with their children (Acts 2: 39), and since children of believing parents are within the covenant of God's mercy, most of the churches of Christendom practise infant Baptism. This is the sacrament of the prevenient (going before) love of God. It tells us in a marvellous way of God's fatherly care for His children.

St. Paul implies that by Baptism we are sealed "with the promised Holy Spirit" (Eph. 1: 13; 2 Cor. 1: 22). Water and the Spirit are linked together in both the Gospels and the Epistles (e.g., John 3: 5; 1 John 5: 6). Baptism is thus the outward sign of an inner grace which God gives through the Spirit.

Further, Baptism is invariably connected with the death of Christ (e.g., Rom. 6: 3; Col. 2: 12). By means of Baptism, St. Paul teaches in Romans (chapter 6), we participate in Christ's death and triumph. Such a relationship between Baptism and Christ's reconciling sacrifice is also found in Revelation (1: 5), Titus (2: 11), and other New Testament passages. In other words, it is Christ who saves and the sign of His saving grace is Baptism (1 Cor. 6: 11). And when we think of the objective efficacy of Christ's reconciliation and of how man, whether child or adult, is the recipient of His reconciling work, we believe that there is nothing that so objectifies and sets forth man's helplessness and God's power to save as the practice of infant Baptism.

(iv) *The Lord's Supper.* The Lord's Supper is a means by which we are continually nourished on the Bread of Life. Here at His Table Christ ministers to us through the Spirit. This is supremely the sacrament of fellowship and when we break bread together on our knees we share with Him and with one another the treasures of His Kingdom.

The Lord's Supper is:

(a) An act of *commemoration*. "Do this in remembrance of Me," (1 Cor. 11: 24) said Christ. This is an act of remembering what happened long ago in history when in the Upper Room and on the cross we see Christ's anguish for the sin of the world. But more, we are also remembering that the same Christ is present now as the living Lord, bringing to us the wealth of His mercy.

(b). The Lord's Supper is an act of *communion*. Christ calls us to Himself at His table. We are invited to come in His Name. Every sincere participant knows in his heart that He communes with Christ by means of the bread and the cup. And when we receive the symbols of His broken body and shed blood, we realize that they help to make real to us how great was the cost and how wonderful was the emancipation involved in man's redemption.

(c). At the Lord's Table we enter into an act of *consecration*. "Here we offer and present unto Thee, O Lord, ourselves, our souls and bodies, to be a reasonable, holy and living sacrifice unto Thee." Here we make a responsive offering of ourselves to that love wherewith He has loved us. Here we give ourselves to Him in consecration as we recall that He gave His all for us.

(d). The Lord's Supper also looks forward to the *consummation* of the Kingdom. "Until He comes" (1 Cor. 11: 26) are three words that convey to the believer the certainty that Christ will triumph; that all enemies will finally be cast down and Christ be acknowledged as Lord of all; that sin and death will be banished forever and the Kingdom of God come in its fulness and its glory. Thus at His Table we wait in expectation, and from His Table we go forth to labour in hope, knowing that the future belongs to Him before whom "every knee should bow and every tongue confess that Jesus Christ is Lord, to the glory of God the Father" (Phil. 2: 10, 11).

FOR FURTHER READING

The Household of God, by Lesslie Newbigin
The Nature and Mission of the Church, by Donald G. Miller
The Blessing of the Holy Spirit, by J. E. Fison
The Theology of the Sacraments, by D. M. Baillie
The Means of Grace, by Arthur G. Reynolds

CHAPTER SIX

QUESTIONS FOR DISCUSSION

1 *Is there any relationship between the Christian hope and our hopes for the success of the United Nations in promoting peace?*

2 *Are there any signs of the coming of the Kingdom in our time?*

3 *How can belief in Christ's return help a social worker who is trying to overcome the evils she finds in the slums of a city?*

4 *"You people create your own intellectual problems by thinking about life after death. I don't." This statement was made by a University professor, an atheist, to a group of S.C.M. students. How would you answer the professor?*

5 *Isn't belief in the Last Judgment out of date?*

6 *Should we not think and strive for a better life on earth, rather than concentrate our attention on eternal life?*

7 *Should the Church teach the fear of hell so as to scare people into living the good life?*

8 *If the triumphant Kingdom is to "come down from heaven" and our efforts have nothing to do with its coming, why do we work for its realization in this world of time?*

9 *Should we pray for the dead?*

10 *Do you think that the saints in heaven are sufficiently concerned about us on earth that, like Christ, they "intercede" on our behalf?*

11 *Can the culture and religion of our day supply better images than those found, say in the Book of Revelation, to depict the life of the world to come? Can our scientific thinking help us here?*

12 *Why has Spiritualism (communication with the dead) always been regarded as heretical by the Church?*

90

Consummation

1 / INTRODUCTION

We have surveyed the content of the gospel from the initial revelation of God to the fellowship of Christ's Church, indwelt by the Holy Spirit. But a question, which is also part of the gospel's content, still remains to be answered. What is the end of it all? What is the goal toward which the action of redemption has been moving? What is the final out-working of God's purpose? In other words, what is the consummation (bringing to perfection or completion) of the work of grace?

We must note at the outset of this discussion of "last things" that all that a Christian can say regarding life after death and the consummation of the Kingdom is definitely related to what has already been said about the resurrection of Christ in Chapter Four. Apart from His resurrection we have very little to declare about the end of history and the final summing up of this earthly scheme of things. But in His resurrection we have a foretaste, a sign of promise, of what is to come, when God will gather all things together in Christ, whose reign shall have no end.

2 / THE CHRISTIAN HOPE

The shadow of death lies over all of man's life and achievements. But the problem presented by death is more than the problem of human survival. It is the problem of the survival of those values which man incarnates and which he believes are of eternal worth; it is the problem of the triumph of righteousness over evil; it is the problem of life's meaning and purpose and of the continuance of the good society of love. Therefore it is important that the Church should have something positive to say to man about the End. Death is truly man's "last enemy," and though man may triumph over his other enemies, if he cannot win the victory over this one he and his world of values are doomed to destruction and oblivion in the great void of a friendless universe. How necessary, then, that the Church should have a message of hope to offer men!

The Second Assembly of the World Council of Churches, meeting in Evanston in 1954, took as its theme: "Christ, the Hope of the World." It was soon apparent, however, that the people of God in our time were not very sure what they meant by the Christian hope. The term had become so secularized, so identified with progress and man's wishes for tomorrow, that its religious depth and its biblical orientation had been obscured. One of the achievements of the Evanston Assembly was that it forced the Church to re-think the Christian hope and its meaning for our day, and to base its thinking on a renewed study of God's revelation in Christ.

Since the Christian hope is centered in Christ—crucified, risen and ascended—there is a certainty about it which should never disappoint us. This hope does not depend on our wishing or willing. It has an objective ground in Him Who is our Lord and Who by His triumph over death has given us a vision of the victorious End God has in store for His people and creation. His victory over evil is the pledge which gives certainty to the Christian hope that the day will come when Christ will be acknowledged as Lord of all and His Church will serve Him in peace.

3 / THE KINGDOM OF GOD

The King has a Kingdom. At the beginning of His ministry in Galilee Jesus proclaimed the Kingdom of God (Mark 1: 15).

That is, He announced the rule or reign of God (which is the primary meaning of this term "Kingdom"), though this rule cannot be separated from its secondary meaning of the realm over which He rules. Since God reigns it was, therefore, with a new sense of urgency that Jesus made this announcement about the Kingdom at the beginning of His ministry, as well as throughout the record of those three short years.

Jesus declared that the Kingdom was present in His own life and work. "If it is by the finger of God that I cast out demons, then the Kingdom of God is come upon you," said Jesus (Luke 11: 20). He also told His disciples that the Kingdom of God "is in the midst of you" (Luke 17: 21). This tells us that the Kingdom is a present reality. Where God's power is manifest there is to be seen the presence of the Kingdom. And Jesus embodies the powers of the Kingdom in His own life. In Him the Kingdom is incarnate.

But the Kingdom has only been realized in part. We learn from the doxology at the end of the Lord's Prayer that "Thine is the Kingdom", but we are also taught in that same prayer to pray, "Thy Kingdom come." In other words, while realizing that in some measure the Kingdom is here, Jesus taught us to pray for its complete manifestation. This implies that the Kingdom has dimensions which extend into the future. By our obedience in faith and prayer and service we set up tokens of God's rule among men. By our obedience we receive the revelation of the Kingdom and announce to men that God reigns. By our obedience, we affirm that the partial realization of the Kingdom in history is integrally related to the coming of the Kingdom in eternity.

Further, the Kingdom is both "this-worldly" and "other-worldly." It was while He was on earth that Jesus announced the presence of the Kingdom. His deeds of mercy, for example, were evidence of its power among men. But the source of the Kingdom's power was not to be found in this world of time. That source was in an eternal world which eye has not seen, except the eye of faith.

Again, the coming of the Kingdom is both personal and social. It is only within the context of the Kingdom, or God's rule, that man comes to His full personal stature. But he cannot do this as a solitary individual. Personality grows and matures in community. Salvation cannot be ours except our brethren be with us. Hence the emphasis on the Church as the instrument of the Kingdom and the vehicle of the Kingdom's power, which must be part and parcel of the gospel we declare.

But the note that must be sounded concerning the Kingdom is the certainty of its coming in power and glory. It is evident that as things are "we do not yet see everything in subjection to him (Christ). But we see Jesus . . . crowned with glory and honour because of the suffering of death, so that by the grace of God he might taste death for every one" (Heb. 2: 9). In other words, to make use of Oscar Cullmann's imagery, D-day has arrived although V-day is still to come. D-day was the day of decision because it was on that day when the Normandy beaches were taken by the Allied Forces, that the decisive battle of World War II was fought and won, even though the War continued for nearly a year afterwards. So the death, resurrection and ascension of Christ is like D-day. He has won the decisive battle for His people. There are still some mopping up operations to be carried out in the interim before V-day. But V-day will surely come. The victory of Christ on D-day is the pledge of His final triumph on V-day. And in the interim we are to witness to His victory, and proclaim the glad tidings that Christ's Kingdom is coming, and will come, in power and glory. This hope, which purifies us in our pilgrimage, is based on our faith in Jesus Christ.

4 / THE RETURN OF CHRIST

The chief symbol or image by which the New Testament depicts the consummation of the Kingdom is that of the return or second advent of Christ. This is sometimes spoken of as "His appearing," or "the revelation," or "the day" of Christ (*e.g.* 2

Thess. 2: 8; 1 Tim. 6: 14; 2 Tim. 1: 10; 1 Peter 1: 6, 7; 4: 13; 1 Cor. 1: 8).

Jesus said that not even He, but only the Father (Mark 13: 32), knew when the Kingdom would be triumphant. Yet it is certain that Jesus believed in its triumphant consummation and in His own return as a prominent part of it (Mark 13: 21). Hence His counsel to "watch." Even in those portions of the New Testament which apparently teach a "realized eschatology" (from the Greek *eschaton,* meaning "last things"), which may be better described as an "inaugurated eschatology," the writers also teach Christ's second advent (*e.g.,* John 14: 3; Col. 3: 3, 4; 1 Peter 1: 7).

The phrase "the return of Christ" is highly symbolic language but it represents a reality, namely, that the Kingdom of which Christ is King will come to an end, a climax, in power and glory; that Christ the Redeemer will have the last word, even as He already has had the first word to say about creation (Heb. 11: 3); that all His enemies will be cast out of God's world for "He must reign" (1 Cor. 15: 25).

"Faith in Jesus Christ without the expectation of His Parousia (Second Coming) is a voucher that is never redeemed, a promise that is not seriously meant. A Christian faith without expectation of the Parousia is like a ladder which leads nowhere but ends in the void."[1] No amount of re-thinking of the Christian message and Christian imagery (de-mythologizing) in the New Testament should be permitted to obscure this important aspect of the gospel. No corruptions of this doctrine should hide from us the tremendous truth which this teaching contains. For in this picture of the return of Christ we have symbolized in an event the altogether important truth, upon which our faith depends, that God will be victorious over all opposition to His reign and His Kingdom come and His will be done in earth as it is in Heaven.

Moreover, the consummation of the Kingdom by our Lord's return reminds us that the coming of the Kingdom is not man's doing—it is the Lord's. Its consummation is His achievement,

[1]Emil Brunner, *Eternal Hope,* p. 138.

not ours. It is a work of grace all the way. We may build our civilizations but the Kingdom does not come as a necessary sequence to many centuries of human progress. The consummation is a crisis event, it is the breaking in of God's eternal order into our temporal order in a new way. Man by his sin may delay the Kingdom's coming; he may for a time obstruct the purposes of God. But he cannot defeat God's will.

Again, the promise of the return of Christ assures us that the future belongs to Him. In this day of confusion in human affairs we are tempted to believe that God is no longer in control of His world, that Jesus Christ is not Lord over all. But the writers of the New Testament also lived in disturbing times in which their faith was tested severely. Rome was sovereign mistress of the world and all peoples obeyed her authority. But on Patmos, John, a prisoner of Rome, could see that the future did not belong to Rome and its persecuting emperor *but to Him Who is Lord* of Lords and King of Kings (Rev. 17: 14). No earthly monarch and no evil that man can do can hinder Christ from bringing to His own conclusion that which He has purposed to do, to reconcile the world unto Himself through the bringing in of His Kingdom. Because of what He has accomplished through His first coming we have faith to believe that Christ will bring to completion in His Second Coming.

It is faith in the second advent of Christ and the consummation of the Kingdom He will bring with Him which serves as a "rod and staff" to Christians in days of adversity. The chariot of history moves on into the future, but because of our belief in Christ we know that the One who commands that chariot is not some unknown demon, nor any human power, but the Christ Who is Lord. "Beloved, we are God's children now; it does not yet appear what we shall be, but we know that when He appears we shall be like Him, for we shall see Him as He is. And every one who thus hopes in Him purifies himself as He is pure" (1 John 3: 2, 3).

There is no more purifying, sanctifying and strengthening

factor in the Christian gospel than this belief in the second coming of Christ. We recognize that sometimes this doctrine has been corrupted by those who desire to draft some celestial time-table and fall into the heresy of converting the eschatological into the merely historical. As a result some Christians have revolted against the doctrine altogether. But such corruptions of what is essentially a teaching of singular significance in Christianity ought not to prevent us from finding and proclaiming the positive values to be found in the truth of the second advent. The closing prayer of the Bible ought to be the prayer of the whole Church in its earthly pilgrimage: "Come, Lord Jesus" (Rev. 22: 20).

In a world where armies of ideas and ideologies clash by day as well as by night, and in a time when men's hearts are failing them for fear of what may be coming on the earth—in such a time we ought to listen for the note of hope and encouragement which belief in the second coming gives to devout souls, as set forth in the final message of the Evanston Assembly of the World Council of Churches: "We are not sufficient for these things. But Christ is sufficient. We do not know what is coming to us. But we know Who is coming. It is He Who meets us every day and Who will meet us at the end—Jesus Christ our Lord. Therefore we say to you: Rejoice in hope."

5 / THE LAST JUDGMENT

Our Lord tells us that one of the purposes involved in His second coming and the establishment of His Kingdom is to conduct the final or last judgment (Matt. 25: 31-46). This judgment must be conceived not merely in terms of condemnation but also of approbation. Judgment is a crisis event, the sifting of the wheat from the chaff, the dividing of the sheep from the goats.

It is certain that because we live in a morally ordered world judgment as a process is going on all the time. The prophetic message of the Old Testament is very strong on this point. But this message, which was taken over by Jesus in His call to repentance, also stresses the fact that evil would have its culmination and wickedness would reach a climax. This truth is underscored by the picture of the final wars with evil in the book of Revelation.

In addition to the parable of the judgment in Matthew 25, there are other parables told by Jesus which set forth the fact of a crisis in human life leading to judgment, such as the parable of the wise and foolish virgins, the parable of the talents (Matt. 25: 1-30) and the teaching of the New Testament generally which states in various ways that "we shall all stand before the judgment seat of God" (Rom. 14: 10).

By means of the judgment and the sifting of the good from the evil there will be a recognition of true worth by Christ, the vindication of love and the establishment of God's order. To some degree this is taking place now. But the doctrine of the last judgment tells us of a grand finale in judgment, when everything is taken into account and final decisions are made by Him Who is the rightful judge of all.

The symbol of the last judgment is not a very acceptable one in our day. In an age in which the cross is still a stumbling-block to the legalist and a thing of sheer folly to the rationalist, it ought not to be surprising that the crisis of judgment between good and evil should lead many to deny all thought of divine judgment here or hereafter. Our humanism and sentimentalism have led men to deny the gospel of redemption of which one element is judgment.

So the question is: How shall we recover this essential note of judgment in our faith? Not by preaching judgment per se. It must come by declaring the reality of God in Christ and the content of this revelation—a God Who is holy, moral love; a God whose highest manifestation is in the crisis of Calvary with its sifting power. It is by bringing men to see the fulness of God's revelation of Himself and His Kingdom that we can recover the emphasis on judgment in Christianity.

6 / THE FINAL DESTINY OF THE RIGHTEOUS

(i) *Eternal Life.* We are told that at the last judgment "the righteous (go) into eternal life" (Matt. 25: 46). This is the state of blessedness reserved for those who have believed in Christ and have been faithful to Him. It does not begin on the other side of death. Eternal life is to be found through faith in Christ while one is on earth. "This is eternal life, that they know thee, the only true God, and Jesus Christ whom thou has sent" (John 17: 3).

According to this definition, eternal life is not primarily life that never ends but life that has a certain quality, the quality which comes through communion with God in Christ. Such a life is eternal because it participates in the life of the eternal God. It is life for both this world and the next because death cannot sever the communion of the believer with his Lord. In the world to come eternal life finds its fulfilment in the consummation of the Kingdom.

This view of eternal life implies that there is no long interval between death and entrance upon the fuller life of the world to come. If life for the righteous is eternal we cannot conceive of any great gap in this life, though crises are not to be ruled out, especially the chief crisis of the final judgment when those who are truly righteous will receive our Lord's approbation, "Well done." This view that there is no long interval, no dwelling in some sort of limbo after death, would appear to be in accord with our Lord's teaching. When Martha said to Him, "I know that he (Lazarus) will rise again in the resurrection at the last day," Jesus said to her, "I am the resurrection and the life; he who believes in me shall never die" (John 11: 24-26). It is also in accord with the mature thought of St. Paul (See 2 Cor. 5: 1-10).

Eternal life is an "inheritance," a gift through the power and love of the risen and ascended Lord. Man cannot achieve it; neither can he merit it. He can only accept it thankfully and regard himself thereafter as a debtor to eternal love.

(ii) *Heaven*. Those who experience eternal life live in heaven, the state or condition of those who are with God. Heaven is where Christ is, the author of true beatitude (John 14: 3). In heaven believers are in the society of the redeemed and experience the fulness of the communion of saints.

What kind of a life will it be for those who have gone to heaven? Dogmatism must be ruled out here, but we know that the life of heaven is a life of real personal existence, a life with Christ and the saints. It is not a disembodied life, for it is one in which the believers possess spiritual bodies given them by God, that is, bodies suitable for the life of heaven. In 1 Corinthians 15 St. Paul uses many terms to describe this heavenly existence: the saints have bodies of incorruption, immortality, glory, power—terms which indicate that a wonderful transformation has taken place by the grace of God.

Further, since the life of heaven is a life of real persons there is no doubt that personal identity will remain. For how could there be a communion of saints without recognition of oneself and others?

Heaven will also be a "life of progressive development" in character and service. "His servants shall worship (serve) him" (Rev. 22: 3). Only through such development can personality mature and only by means of such service as He will give us can we experience the beatitude of heaven. While the saints "will rest from their labors" (Rev. 14: 13), they will not be idle. Their deeds follow with them not only in their good influence left behind on earth but even more in the unselfish habits and mode of life that were acquired in the service of Christ on earth.

Here we walk by faith and not by sight. But faith gives us second sight, an inner realization of the wonders of the heavenly state. Its first fruits are given to us through communion with the Holy Spirit, who is the earnest of things to come. "What no eye has seen, nor ear heard, nor the heart of man conceived, what God has prepared for those who love Him, God has revealed to us through the Spirit" (1 Cor. 2: 9, 10).

7/THE FINAL DESTINY OF THE UNRIGHTEOUS

While the main teaching of the New Testament respecting man's final destiny concerns the destiny of the righteous, nevertheless there are some things which must be said about the final destiny of the unrighteous. On this matter the Bible is very reticent and we must not press biblical images into dogmas.

In Church history we can discover three broad points of view on the final destiny of the unrighteous:

(a) *Universalism.* According to this view all men, righteous and wicked, will ultimately be saved. Since God is love it would be impossible for Him to permit even one soul to remain outside His Kingdom, so at the last, perhaps after a process of purgation in the next world (like purgatory), all will be brought to the knowledge of the truth as it is in Jesus.

Aside from the fact that any doctrine of purgatory is not biblical (Roman Catholics base their view of purgatory largely on passages in the Apocrypha) and that it is definitely connected theologically with the doctrine of merit which a religion of grace must repudiate, the weaknesses of universalism can easily be detected: (i) It does not take seriously the warnings of Jesus about the "outer darkness" and the fact of moral retribution, whereby a man is punished by his sins, if not for them. (ii) Universalism overlooks the fact that the more one persists in sin, the more his heart becomes hardened to the call to repent.

(iii) Sin is deeply embedded in human life and if a man, lost in sin, persists in refusing God's grace, not even God can compel him to enter the Kingdom. (iv) "It is illogical to tell men that they must do the will of God and accept His gospel of grace, if you also tell them that the obligation has no eternal significance, and that nothing ultimately depends on it."[2] (v) Universalism tends to sentimentalism because it treats lightly the demands of God's love with respect to obedience to the moral law.

[2]John S. Whale, *Christian Doctrine*, p. 186.

(b) *Conditionalism.* This position, reflecting the teaching of the "survival of the fittest" in the world of science, states that only those who are "fit" to survive do so. All others are blotted out by death. That is, only those who inherit eternal life survive the crisis of death. All the rest of humanity perishes in the dust. This view takes Jesus' teaching about "the unquenchable fire" (Luke 3: 17) and St. Paul's reference to "death" as being sin's wages (Rom. 6: 23) and similar passages as a basis in scripture for this position.

Although this view has much to commend it, it has some very serious weaknesses. For instance, who ever is "fit" for the Kingdom? We enter the Kingdom by the mercy of God. No one ever achieves the resurrection. It is God's gift through Christ. Moreover, both "fire" and "death" are images of separation from God and may not necessarily imply destruction. Further, we must not press too far analogies from the world of sciene to represent to us the condition of those not "in Christ" after death.

(c) *Hell.* This is the doctrine of eternal punishment. Our English word "hell" is a translation of such terms as *Sheol, Hades,* and *Gehenna. Sheol* was a Hebrew word, while *Hades* was Greek. These terms denoted the place of the departed who lived in the land "of the shadow of death." It was the place of the "shades", the country of "forgetfulness." In early times, however, neither *Sheol* nor *Hades* was connected with the thought of punishment. *Gehenna* (Matt. 5: 22; Luke 12: 5) was a reference originally to the Valley of Hinnom outside Jerusalem where there was a refuse heap and a fire burned continually to consume the refuse. This became a picture, in the course of time, of the punishment of the wicked. It should also be noted that in late pre-Christian Jewish history Sheol was divided into two parts, one for the righteous, called "paradise," and the other for the wicked, called "Gehenna." This separation of the righteous from the wicked in the after-life was especially prominent in the inter-testamental period in Jewish history.

"Hell" is a symbol, and while it stands for some dread moral reality we must not make it into a place of physical punishment. What we do know is that the way of righteousness leads to heaven and the way of sin leads to separation from God. It is in the latter sense that we must think of hell. Sin has terrible consequences. The cross tells us that. We also know that God does not will the death of a sinner but that all should turn unto Him and live. There may be some way, unknown to us, within the providence of God whereby He can honour man's freedom and at the same time bring man to repentance. There is nothing in the Bible, however, which would lead us to believe that we can presume on God's love in such a manner as to leave the impression on people's minds that everything "will turn out all right in the end." When men persist in saying "No" to God they condemn themselves. What this condemnation involves we can only dimly comprehend.

Question 46 of the Catechism of The United Church of Canada asks: "What does the future hold for those who reject His (God's) redeeming love?" The reply to this question is one of the best answers we can give to this baffling problem of the final destiny of the wicked: "Those who reject His redeeming love shut themselves out from the favour and fellowship of God and His people, a future dark beyond our powers to conceive."

8 / THE CONSUMMATION OF THE KINGDOM

It is not in thoughts concerning the final destiny of the unrighteous that we are able to see the consummation of the Kingdom but in pictures of the state of the blessed and the new order of life which God will bring with Him.

The one Church of Jesus Christ has two aspects: the Church militant on earth, striving by grace to do God's will; and the Church triumphant, in which the redeemed in heaven chant His praise. And the consummation of the Kingdom will come when the Church militant ceases to be and the Church triumphant enjoys the beatitude of the saints. Then "the Kingdom of the

world has become the Kingdom of our Lord and of His Christ, and He shall reign forever and ever" (Rev. 11: 15).

What will be the manner of life in the Kingdom of God at the consummation? We can only use pictures, or analogies drawn from the realm of present human experience, to describe the life of the Kingdom of God when Christ shall be all in all. Here the picture-language of the book of Revelation, with its appeal to the devout imagination, helps us to understand by faith the content of the beatific vision. In chapter 7 we learn that life in the Kingdom has a place for worship and praise, the adoration of the Most High and the consequent joy of the redeemed. "They also serve Him night and day in his temple" (v. 15). The blessed are free from such earthly, physical needs as food and water, and the days of mourning are ended. Again, in Revelation 21 we have another series of pictures of the state of eternal blessedness. It consists of "a new heaven and a new earth." It comes down from God out of heaven and is, therefore, not the product of human achievement (vv. 1, 2). God dwells with His people forever. He has abolished pain, tears and death. That which characterises this state of blessedness is its *newness*.

In Revelation 22 we are further told that the beatific vision will be realized by the saints because "they shall see his face" and the fruit of Christ's reconciling love will be seen in "the healing of the nations." What a blessed event that will be!

All these truths are set forth in the language that appeals to the imagination, not to the reason. But they are not "vain imaginings." They are pictures that depict in symbolic terms the tremendous spiritual realities which will be understood by those who have already tasted the powers of the age to come through their faith in the Lord Jesus Christ.

We learn from the Bible, interpreted through the mind of Christ, that God's purpose in creation, redemption and sanctification is "to create a community of persons endowed with genuine freedom"[3] and able to have fellowship with Him and with one

---

[3]Leonard Hodgson, *Christian Theology*, Vol. II, "For Faith and Freedom,"p. 61.

another. It is the realization of this purpose that we find in the pictures of the consummation of the Kingdom in the book of Revelation. "Behold, the dwelling of God is with men. He will dwell with them, and they shall be his people, and God himself shall be with them" (Rev. 21: 3).

Further, the consummation is not only for men; it is universal in its reference. For although now "the whole creation waits with eager longing for the revealing of the sons of God" (Rom. 8: 19), when the Kingdom comes in all its fulness and glory "the creation itself will be set free from its bondage to decay and obtain the glorious liberty of the children of God" (Rom. 8: 21). Freedom for man and creation, freedom from sin and evil and death—it is this which is given by God when His Kingdom is consummated in glory. And when the Kingdom comes in power there will be ushered in the perfected life of man with God when the beatific vision will be a reality, for not only will the saints "see his face" but "his name" shall also "be on their foreheads" (Rev. 22: 4). Such is the intimacy of the communion of the faithful with their Lord in that Golden Age of the Kingdom.

One final word. This is all the Lord's doing. Man has not achieved it. By faith he receives it through grace. By the mercy of God he enters the blessedness of His Kingdom. Therefore the Church triumphant sings: "Worthy is the Lamb who was slain to receive power and wealth and wisdom and might and honour and glory and blessing" (Rev. 5: 12). Amen and Amen!

FOR FURTHER READING

Life After Death, by J. M. Shaw

Life and Death, issued by the Committee on Christian Faith of The United Church of Canada

The Christian Hope: the Presence and the Parousia, by J. E. Fison

Christian Hope and the Second Coming, by Paul S. Minear

Eternal Hope, by Emil Brunner

The Kingdom of God, by John Bright

CHAPTER SEVEN

QUESTIONS FOR DISCUSSION

1 *Should the Church endeavour to persuade people of other faiths to believe in Jesus Christ? Why?*

2 *Should modern missions concentrate on taking medicine, education, etc., to people in needy lands, without an emphasis on evangelism?*

3 *Can you think of any new elements in strategy that should be adopted by the Church in its mission?*

4 *Is Christ's authority sufficient motivation for the Church to carry on her missionary enterprise today?*

5 *What is involved in being a disciple of Jesus Christ? What, for instance, distinguishes a Christian from a Moslem?*

6 *What new teaching methods should the Church adopt in order to educate her people in the Christian faith?*

7 *"Missionary obligation is the life-blood of the Christian faith" (J. S. Thomson). Why?*

8 *How does Jesus call disciples today?*

9 *"Love to Christ for what he has done for us is the deepest ingredient in the motivation to mission" (Donald G. Miller). Why?*

10 *How can we get more unity in mission among the churches?*

11 *What must the CHURCH, which already believes in Christ, do to be saved?*

Commission

1 / MAN'S NEED OF REDEMPTION

In her drama, *The Man Born to be King*,[1] Dorothy L. Sayers introduces to King Herod three kings from afar: Caspar, Melchior and Balthazar. These kings tell him that a special star has appeared in the heavens, an augury that a great king is about to be born. They have come to ask King Herod where he is to be born. Herod is disturbed. He is old and feeble but he wants no rival king in his domain under Caesar. The following conversation takes place:

Herod: Tell me this? Will he be a warrior King?

Balthazar: The greatest of warriors; yet he shall be called the Prince of Peace. He will be victor and victim in all his wars, and will make his triumph in defeat. And when his wars are over, he will rule his people in love.

Herod: You cannot rule men by love. When you find your King tell him so. Only three things will govern a people—fear and greed and the promise of security.

Unfortunately it is still to a large extent true that men are governed by fear and greed and the promise of security. When we think how men respond to such appeals in our time and how

[1]Play 1, Scene 1.

some have gained power over multitudes by using such appeals, we must realize afresh that man needs to be redeemed from these and other sins which so easily beset him. For these three things which according to Herod govern a people are evidence of the demonic character in human life from which Christ came to deliver us.

William Penn stated that "men will ultimately be ruled either by tyrants or by God." Herod makes the tyrant's appeal—and he gains his ends. We within the Church have also an appeal to make on God's behalf. "We are ambassadors for Christ, God making his appeal through us. We beseech you on behalf of Christ, be reconciled to God" (2 Cor. 5: 20).

2 / THE RESPONSIBILITY OF THE CHURCH

It is the claim of the Church that the Christian gospel has the final answer to the problem of man's sin and its consequences of fear, greed and the promise of security. We believe that the gospel offers the perfect love which casts out fear, the grace of Jesus Christ which banishes greed, and a victorious faith in Him who has conquered sin and death: faith which gives man the only ultimate security he can find.

We Christians have this glorious and precious treasure in our keeping—the gift of God to us in the gospel. But it is not for our keeping; it is for our sharing. It is for us to pass on to others that they may see and believe and that they may be truly delivered from the kingdom of darkness to the Kingdom of God's dear Son. And to this end we have been given our marching orders. The army of the Lord has an offensive to undertake for Him. We must go into all the world and offer men the unsearchable riches of Christ, to the end that men may believe in the gospel and find eternal life. This is a glorious privilege. It is also an awe-inspiring responsibility.

Many reasons may be advanced why the Church should undertake this responsibility of proclaiming the gospel to all the world and carry on the work of evangelism which began long ago in

Galilee. There is, for example, the obvious need of mankind for salvation. Then there is the motive of Christ's love which bids us share His truth with others. Moreover, since we believe He is Lord of all we cannot refrain from proclaiming His lordship to all men. However, we believe that the words of Jesus usually called the Great Commission are in themselves a good summary of many reasons why the Church must evangelize the world and, in addition, these words of our Lord lay a constraint on us to do as He would have us do for His sake. "All authority in heaven and on earth has been given to me. Go therefore and make disciples of all nations," spake the risen Christ, "baptizing them in the name of the Father and of the Son and of the Holy Spirit, teaching them to observe all that I have commanded you; and lo, I am with you always, to the close of the age" (Matt. 28: 18-20).

3 / THE AUTHORITY OF CHRIST

The first thing we must note about this Great Commission is that we are asked to obey it under the authority of Christ Himself. We are commissioned to go and make disciples not by the Church but by Him Who is the Head of the Church. "All authority in heaven and on earth" has been given to the living Christ. The initial decision whether we should evangelize the world is not ours, therefore, but Christ's. He calls. We must obey. Hesitancy and indifference to His call merely show our own indecision.

The fields are white unto harvest. Sin is still paying the wages of death. Men are lost in the darkness of superstition, idolatry and selfishness. If we believe the good news that has been given to us, how can we keep it to ourselves? How can we refrain from offering men the gospel of salvation? When we really believe the gospel we are constrained to pass it on.

Moreover, since Christ has all authority, He Himself is the chief evangelist, as the Evanston Report of the World Council of Churches on Evangelism pointed out. We are Christ's instru-

ments in evangelism. We can convert no one ourselves. Christ
uses us to bring others to a saving knowledge of God's love. Like
good ambassadors, therefore, we do not go with our own message
but with that which has been given to us by our King. Our
credentials are from Him and Him alone. Moreover, like true
ambassadors, we must be faithful to our King and to the task
He has assigned us. "It is required of stewards that they be found
trustworthy" (1 Cor. 4: 2).

The authority which Christ exercises over us as He commissions
us is that of divine love. What sort of love this is we can see at
Calvary. It is the love that was crucified for us, the love that
went beyond the second mile and the third mile, the love that
gave its all. Henceforth we know that we have been sacrificed
for; we have "been bought with a price" (1 Cor. 6: 20).

There is no authority in heaven or on earth that can so constrain people to serve and sacrifice as the authority of sacrificial
love. Ethical commands may cause us to go so far in obedience;
love causes us to go all the way. When love takes hold of our
hearts we set no limits to what we will or will not do.

4 / THE CHURCH MUST MAKE DISCIPLES

We see in the words of the Great Commission the purpose
of the Church's life and work—to make disciples of all nations.
Mission is of the essence of the Church's existence. She has no
other reason for continuing in the world but that of making
disciples for Christ. Worship and praise, fellowship and service
are meant to do more than edify us or even glorify God. Their
purpose is also to equip the saints with a sense of mission so
that they may carry out the task God has given them and in this
way also glorify His Name. Mission is, therefore, of both the
being and the well-being of the Church.

In carrying out the Great Commission the Church does not
go to others to dominate or coerce, or to boast about superior
knowledge and culture. We go as disciples to share Christ's truth
and thus under Him make disciples. We go as those who have

found Him Who has brought life and immortality to light through His gospel and we say, in effect, "Here is life and light for you; here is forgiveness for sin and the freedom of the saints; here is Christ who emancipates from guilt," for "there is therefore now no condemnation for those who are in Christ Jesus" (Rom. 8: 1). "The new spiritual principle of life in Christ Jesus" can lift you "out of the old vicious circle of sin and death" (Rom. 8: 2, J. B. Phillips translation). So we have found Christ to mean to us and the Church, and we declare to others that He can mean the same to them.

When we have experienced Christ's redeeming love we go forth to share His love with others. Only in this way can we make disciples. God uses us to manifest His marvellous grace. And in some way beyond our understanding, when we are obedient and faithful, in spite of our weakness and failure, His light shines through to others and men believe.

5 / THE FOURFOLD MISSION OF THE CHURCH

The mission of the Church has a fourfold pattern:

(a) *It is priestly.* A priest is an intermediary between the people and their God. Christ is our Great High Priest (Heb. 4: 14) Who intercedes for men (Heb. 7: 25), Who has made the "one, perfect and sufficient sacrifice for the sins of the whole world (Heb. 9: 26) and Who has created for Himself a Body, the Church, which is a "holy priesthood," set apart "to offer spiritual sacrifices acceptable to God through Jesus Christ" (1 Peter 2: 5). The Church, therefore, under the Headship of Christ, has a priestly ministry to perform, namely, to lead men in the worship of the true God, to teach them of the Saviour Who sacrificed Himself for them, and to offer spiritual sacrifices for others by means of prayer and service.

(b) *It is prophetic.* A prophet is one who speaks forth the Word of the Lord. He calls men to a high moral path. He utters forth the commandments of God. He says, in effect, "This is the way, walk in it" (Is. 30: 21). "Remove the evil of your doings from before my eyes; cease to do evil, learn to do good; seek justice, correct oppression" (Is. 1: 16, 17) is part of the burden of the prophet's message.

In being obedient to her prophetic mission the Church must serve as the conscience of the nation, calling people to forsake evil and follow after that which is righteous and just and good. "And whether they will hear or refuse to hear (for they are a rebellious house) they will know that there has been a prophet among them" (Ez. 2: 5).

(c) *It is redemptive.* Weak and sinful man needs a power other than his own if he is to turn from his wicked ways and find fellowship with God. It is the Christian gospel that God gives man this power through the living Christ and the Spirit's presence. Man is not sufficient to overcome the sins that beset him; but Christ is sufficient for every need of man. By His grace man can be pardoned and restored to newness of life. He can go forth into life knowing that the burden of guilt has been lifted from off his shoulders and the freedom of the sons of God now becomes his precious possession. He is able to unite in doxology with the whole Church, saying, "To Him who loves us and has freed us from our sins by His blood and made us a Kingdom, priests to his God and father, to Him be glory and dominion for ever and ever. Amen" (Rev. 1: 5, 6).

(d) *It is unitive.* The message of the Epistle to the Ephesians is not only the unity of the Church in Christ; it is also the message of God's purpose to unite all things in Him. "For He has made known to us . . . according to His purpose which He set forth in Christ as a plan for the fulness of time, to unite all things in Him, things in heaven and things on earth" (Eph. 1: 9, 10). Since God is love, it is apparent that His purpose is to unite all people in a fellowship of love under Christ. And in a world that is disunited, torn by strife and animosity, prejudice and selfishness, there is greater need for the unity Christ can give than ever before. The present need of men in this respect presents a wonderful opportunity for the Church to proclaim the gospel that Christ "is our peace . . . and has broken down the dividing wall of hostility . . . that He might create in Himself one new man in place of the two, so making peace, and might reconcile us both to God in one body through the cross, thereby bringing the hostility to an end" (Eph. 2: 14-16).

6 / FACTORS IN MAKING DISCIPLES

According to the words of the Great Commission there are three factors involved in making disciples:

(a) *Baptism.* The Church is called to go forth on her mission and baptize in the name of the triune God.

By Baptism the child or adult, as we have seen previously, is admitted into the community of salvation, the Church, where Christ is present in the faith and fellowship of His people; where His blessing comes to the saints; where He cleanses, pardons and sanctifies all who are within His covenant of grace. Baptism is the sign of God's covenanting love, a love that will not let us go and that will not let us down. By this sign of Baptism Christ pledges Himself to His children forever.

Further, Baptism admits a person to that community where there is new hope, new life and a new purpose. Here in the Church the worship of Almighty God is carried on; here prayer and praise are offered to the Most High; here confession of sin is made and pardon received; here one sees the whole of life as under God. Baptism in very truth is the beginning of the greatest adventure upon which anyone can enter—the adventure of being a Christian disciple and following where Christ leads.

(b) *Teaching.* The second factor in making disciples is that of "teaching them to observe all that I have commanded you." The promises made at Baptism can only be fulfilled as the Church remembers her mission to teach those who have been baptized. Only thus can God work His perfect will in the lives of those who have entered the fellowship of God's people.

In this day when "isms" and ideologies of all kinds are around us, it is very important that Christians know whereof they believe. Only by being well-grounded in Christian truth will they be able to witness for Christ and tell of the wonder of His saving grace. It is by means of teaching that the disciples are built up in their most holy faith and have the fortitude to stand in the evil day.

(c) *Christ.* The presence of Christ is the chief factor in making disciples. He wins them and loves them. "Lo, I am with you always, to the close of the age" — "the promise of a gentleman of the most strict and sacred honor," according to David Livingstone.

In fulfilling the Great Commission of our Lord we do not go alone. His promise is that He will never leave us nor forsake us. If we go on our own we are inviting defeat. If we go with Him we know that whatever success we have belongs to Him Who strengthens us, uses us and directs us. He is the one Who in times of discouragement keeps us from falling. He is the One Who supports us all the day long of this troublous life. As Augustine said: "Without us He will not; without Him we cannot."

Alexander Whyte used to say that "the perseverance of the saints depends on the perseverance of the Saviour." That was never more true than in this task of making disciples. It is in such work, which demands perseverance, that Christ's presence is needed in a very special way. Without His lordship and leadership we are working to no end and the result of all our efforts will be null and void as far as the Kingdom of heaven is concerned. As the "pioneer and perfecter of our faith" (Heb. 12: 2) He equips us with a faith sufficient for the mission we are called to undertake for Him.

All three factors are still needed by the Church that is called to make disciples: Baptism to be the sign of God's blessing, the sacramental symbol of a love that reaches out to all Whom God calls; teaching, the continuing and ever-present need of the Church for the instruction and edification of the faithful; and, in and through all the worship and work, faith and life, the presence of Christ without Whom we can do nothing.

7 / COMMUNION, COMMITMENT AND COMMISSION

Since we need Christ's presence to be with us in our life and work we must realize that there must be communion with Him —daily. We must enter into "the shelter of the Most High" and abide "in the shadow of the Almighty" (Ps. 91: 1). It is by communion with Him that we are able to extricate ourselves from the Slough of Despond, climb our Hill Difficulty, pass through Vanity Fair with head erect, fight our way through the Valley of Humiliation, outrun Giant Despair and leave Doubting Castle behind us, and at last enter that city which lies foursquare.

Rufus Jones, in his book, *New Eyes for Invisibles,* tells us that Holman Hunt announced one day to some fellow artists that he was going to paint Christ. They thought that was absurd. A man could paint only what he could see. "But I am going to see Him," replied Hunt. "I will work by His side in the carpenter's shop. I will walk with Him over the hills of Galilee. I will go with Him among the poor, the blind, the naked, the lepers. I will travel with Him to Calvary and climb the cross with Him, until I see Him and know Him, and then I will paint Him." Holman Hunt carried out his purpose and gave us that famous painting "The Light of the world." And as we gaze at that picture of Christ, the crown of thorns on His head, a lantern in one hand and the other raised knocking at the door, we know that only a man who communed with Christ could give the world that masterpiece of religious art.

Communion must lead to commitment in personal dedication to the Lord of all. Without this commitment our communion with Him is likely to degenerate into a sentimental and emotional affair. Without this commitment we are apt to make communion an end in itself, lacking that outreach and dedication which ought to be the hallmark of Christian living. But when we do commit our lives into His hands and go forth to sow with the good seed of the Word we can never tell what great things may happen, since with God all things are possible. The harvest may be thirty fold, sixty fold or even one hundred fold. But our responsibility is that of commitment—and sowing.

John Calvin's famous crest was an open hand of dedication, on which was a flaming heart of zeal and passion for His Lord. Around this crest were Latin words which mean: "My heart I give Thee, Lord, willingly and sincerely." This is the sort of commitment which the Church must demand of all her members if she is to commune with her Lord in sincerity and in truth and to obey our Lord's command to go and make disciples of all nations.

We return again finally to the Great Commission itself. Here is where our communion and our commitment must lead us: to obey Christ and go forth into all the world.

A newspaper reporter visited a Communist leader at his office. He noticed on his desk this motto: "A world to win." Have the Communists stolen the perspective of the gospel from the Christians? We are told that "God so loved the world" (John 3: 16) and we have been commissioned to go into all the world. But to a large degree the Church hangs back while the Communists go in to make disciples with their own secular evangel. In truth, the children of this generation are wiser than the children of light.

Dr. James S. Stewart writes:

Belief in missions and belief in Christ stand and fall together . . . concern for world evangelization is not something tacked on to a man's personal Christianity, which he may take or leave as he chooses: it is rooted indefeasibly in the character of the God who has come to us in Jesus. . . It is the distinctive mark of being a Christian. To accept Christ is to enlist under a missionary banner.

Dr. Stewart goes on to relate that Dr. James Denney once heard a distinguished missionary say—"Some people do not believe in missions. They have no right to believe in missions: they do not believe in Christ."[2]

So it comes to this: do we really believe in Christ? If we do no choice is left to us other than that of obedience to the Great Commission and loyalty to Him Who has called us out of darkness into His marvellous light. Let us, therefore, once again give heed to His words:

All authority in heaven and on earth has been given to me. Go therefore and make disciples of all nations, baptizing them in the name of the Father and of the Son and of the Holy Spirit, teaching them to observe all that I have commanded you; and lo, I am with you always, to the close of the age.

FOR FURTHER READING

Thine Is the Kingdom, by James S. Stewart
The Divine Mission, by James Sutherland Thomson

[2]James S. Stewart, *Thine Is the Kingdom*, p. 14f.

SOURCES OF QUOTATIONS

Baillie, John: *The Idea of Revelation in Recent Thought.* Columbia University Press, New York.

Brunner, Emil: *Eternal Hope.* Westminster Press, Philadelphia, Pa.

Barth, Karl: *Dogmatics in Outline.* S.C.M. Press, London.

Calvin, John: *The Institutes of the Christian Religion.* Westminster Press, Philadelphia, Pa.

Carlyle, Thomas: *Sartor Resartus.* E. P. Dutton & Co., New York.

Coulson, C. A.: *Science and Christian Belief.* University of North Carolina Press, Chapel Hill, N.Y.

The Expositor's Bible. Wm. B. Eerdmans Pub. Co., Grand Rapids, Mich.

Hodgson, Leonard: *Christian Theology.* Charles Scribner's Sons, New York.

Hunter, A. M.: *Introducing New Testament Theology.* Westminster Press, Philadelphia, Pa.

Lewis, C. S.: *Broadcast Talks.* William Collins, Edinburgh.

_____: *The Problem of Pain.* Macmillan Co., New York.

MacKintosh, H. R.: *The Doctrine of the Person of Jesus Christ.* T. & T. Clark, Edinburgh.

Newbigin, L. J.: *The Household of God.* Friendship Press, New York.

Richardson, A. (Ed.): *A Theological Word Book of the Bible.* Macmillan Co., New York.

Sayers, Dorothy L.: *The Man Born to Be King.* Harper & Brothers, New York.

_____: *The Mind of the Maker.* Harcourt Brace & Co., New York.

Sockman, Ralph W.: *How to Believe.* Doubleday & Co. Inc., New York.

Stewart, James S.: *A Faith to Proclaim.* Charbles Scribner's Sons, New York.

_____: *Thine Is the Kingdom.* Charles Scribner's Sons, New York.

Taylor, Vincent: *The Person of Christ.* St. Martins Press Inc., New York.

Temple, William: *Nature, Man and God.* St. Martins Press, Inc., New York.

Thompson, Francis: *Complete Poems.* Modern Library, New York.

Tillich, Paul: *The New Being.* Charles Scribner's Sons, New York.

_____: *Systematic Theology.* University of Chicago Press, Chicago, Ill.

Toynbee, Arnold: *An Historian's Approach to Religion.* Oxford University Press, Fairlawn, N.J.

Whale, John S.: *Christian Doctrine.* Cambridge University Press, New York.